30-SECOND
MYTHOLOGY

30-SECOND
MYTHOLOGY

The 50 most important classical
myths, monsters, heroes, and gods,
each explained in half a minute

Editor
Robert A. Segal

Contributors
Viv Croot
Susan Deacy
Emma Griffiths
William Hansen
Geoffrey Miles
Barry B. Powell
Robert A. Segal

METRO BOOKS
NEW YORK

METRO BOOKS
New York

An Imprint of Sterling Publishing
387 Park Avenue South
New York, NY 10016

This book was conceived,
designed, and produced by
Ivy Press
210 High Street, Lewes,
East Sussex BN7 2NS, U.K.
www.ivy-group.co.uk

Creative Director Peter Bridgewater
Publisher Jason Hook
Editorial Director Caroline Earle
Art Director Michael Whitehead
Designer Ginny Zeal
Illustrator Ivan Hissey
Profiles Text Viv Croot
Glossaries Text Steve Luck
Senior Editor Stephanie Evans
Project Editor Jamie Pumfrey

ISBN-13: 978-1-4351-4066-0

For information about custom editions, special
sales, and premium and corporate purchases,
please contact Sterling Special Sales at 800-805-
5489 or specialsales@sterlingpublishing.com.

Manufactured in China

Color origination by Ivy Press Reprographics

2   4   6   8   10   9   7   5   3   1

www.sterlingpublishing.com

CONTENTS

INTRODUCTION
Robert A. Segal

There is no uniform definition of "myth."

Instead, the numerous definitions reflect the various disciplines that study myths. As surprising as it sounds, a myth need not even be a story. For political scientists, a myth can instead be a belief or credo—an ideology. Even when myth is assumed to be a story, disciplines differ over the content. For folklorists, myths are exclusively about the creation of the world. All other stories constitute either legends or folktales. For other disciplines, myths can also be about the creation of a nation or a movement, or not be about the creation of anything. For the field of religious studies, the main characters in myths must be gods. Other disciplines, however, allow not only for heroes, who are human, but even for animals, who can sometimes be the outright creators of the world.

Three key questions

Many disciplines study myth—the chief ones being anthropology, sociology, psychology, political science, literature, philosophy, and religious studies—and each discipline harbors multiple theories. To theorize about myth is to seek to answer three key questions, and to answer them for all myths, not just for a single myth or the myths of a single culture.

The key questions are those of origin, function, and subject matter. "Origin" addresses why and how myths arise whenever and wherever they do, not when and where they first arose. Function addresses why and how myths persist. The answer to the "why" of both origin and function is usually a need, which the myth arises to fulfil and endures by continuing to fulfil. The need varies from theory to theory.

"Subject matter" addresses what the myth refers to—the "referent." Myths, it is popularly assumed, are to be read literally. Whether or not Zeus was real, myths about Zeus are supposed to be stories of a real god who was the chief god of mainstream, Homeric religion and who

Perseus slays the Gorgon
In one of the best-known heroic quests, Perseus travels to the home of the Gorgon sisters to behead Medusa. These epic tales have endured for centuries and still resonate with a modern audience.

used his power to do as he wished. However, myths can also be read symbolically, and the referent can be anything. Zeus, for example, can symbolize thunder and lightning, a king, a human father, or even the fatherlike side of anyone's personality. Zeus need not be taken as a god, let alone the god of a long dead religion.

Theoretical shifts

Theories not only present myths but also make sense of them. Theories claim to know why myths ever arose, why they lasted for as long as they did, why they may still last, and what they are really "about." One convenient distinction, which cuts across disciplines, is that between theories from the nineteenth century and theories from the twentieth.

Nineteenth-century theories—epitomized by those of E. B. Tylor and J. G. Frazer—usually saw the subject matter of myths as the physical world and the function of myths as either a literal explanation or a symbolic description of that world. Myths were taken to be the "primitive" counterpart to natural science, which was assumed to be wholly or largely modern. Science rendered myths not merely redundant but outright incompatible, and modern audiences, which by definition were scientific, therefore had to reject myths.

By contrast, twentieth-century theories—typified by those of Bronislaw Malinowski, Mircea Eliade, Rudolf Bultmann, Albert Camus, Sigmund Freud, and C. G. Jung—saw myths as anything but an outdated counterpart to science, either in subject matter or in function. (Nineteenth-century theorists like Friedrich Nietzsche foreshadowed this approach.) The subject matter was no longer the physical world but now was society, the human mind, or the place of humans in the physical world. The function of myths was no longer explanation but now ranged from unifying the community, to encountering god, to encountering the unconscious, to expressing the human condition. In short, even in the wake of science, myths still had a place.

Enduring appeal

Did ancient Greeks and Romans believe literally in their mythology? Surprisingly, most did. Modern audiences may not share that literal belief, but the myths have endured and remain celebrated. Even if no one today considers Zeus or Achilles to be real, gods and heroes have flourished as symbols, of whom the grandest example is Dionysus.

Moreover, they have penetrated mainstream thought. Freud used the figure Oedipus to name the most fundamental human male drive, and Jung used the figure Electra to name its female counterpart.

Myths are to be found not only in Christianity and in ancient Greek and Roman religions but in most and maybe all other religions. Furthermore, myths need not be tied to any religion. Twentieth-century theories, in contrast to nineteenth-century ones, often severed myth from religion and studied secular myths, such as myths of nationalism or of outer space. Theories of myth are theories of all myths, not merely of any one culture or of any one kind.

Because classical myths are the best known, they are the focus of *30-Second Mythology*. The Greek, not Latin, names of the gods are used, but familiar Latin, or Roman, names are also given. Each mythological figure or event is first presented in a 30-second mythology, summarizing the key details for the reader, alongside a 3-second muse, which offers a more concise account. The 3-minute odyssey then goes into greater depth, outlining, for example, the symbolism contained within the myth, or further explaining its origin. Finally, related myths reveal the counterparts to mythical figures or events contained within other cultures and civilizations.

The seven chapters are divided into the categories of **Creation**, **Olympians**, **Monsters**, **Geography**, **Heroes**, **Tragic Figures**, and **Legacy**, reflecting the way in which mythology pervades the whole classical world. Not only are there hundreds of gods, about many of whom there are multiple myths, but there also are mythic monsters, locations, and events. The history of the cosmos begins with the creation of gods, who operate continually, often tragically, in the lives of humans. The hundreds of heroes themselves garner myths upon myths. These myths have persisted to this day, one of their legacies being the well-known psychological conditions that take their names from mythic figures.

Classical myths are to be found today in an array of places—not only in literature but also in the arts, the movies, and not least popular culture. Modern versions of ancient myths invariably take liberties with the original stories, but what counts is that the myths, however updated, continue to be told.

CREATION

adamantine sickle From "adamant," which means extremely durable or hard. The most commonly referred to adamantine sickle in classical mythology is that made by Gaia and given to Cronus (Saturn), who used it to castrate his father, Uranus. There are, however, other references to adamantine sickles, such as the one Perseus used to kill Medusa and the sickle with which Zeus defeated Typhon.

cosmogony Derived from the Greek word *kosmos* (literally, "order"), the term refers to the description, often to be found in myth, of the creation of the world.

Giants (Gigantes) The Giants were the huge, often monstrous, mortal male offspring of Gaia. She gave birth to the Giants, having been fertilized by Uranus' blood following his castration by Cronus. When the Olympians imprisoned the Titans, Gaia encouraged the Giants to wage war on Zeus and the other gods, hoping to overthrow them and to restore Titan supremacy. In the ensuing war (the Gigantomachy), Heracles, following a prophecy, was called upon by the gods to fight against the Giants. He personally killed a number of Giants and was responsible for the gods' ultimate victory.

Meliae A sisterhood of ash-tree nymphs (*melia* is Greek for ash), the Meliae, like the Giants and the Erinyes ("Furies"), were Gaia's offspring, fertilized by Uranus' blood. According to Hesiod in his *Works and Days*, the Meliae produced the third race of men, known as the Bronze Race, whom Hesiod described as being "terrible and strong."

Oceanids The collective name given to the many thousand sea nymph offspring of the Titans Oceanus and Tethys. Numbering between 3,000 and 4,000, they were closely associated with the seas and oceans, and many had individual names. Although not immortal, Oceanids lived for a very long time, and generally looked favorably on humans. They were often depicted playing around the keels and prows of boats.

Olympians The term generally refers to the "Twelve Olympians" who gained control of the world after overthrowing the Titans in the war that has become known as the Titanomachy. The main gods of the Greek pantheon, the Twelve Olympians inhabited Mount Olympus, ruled by Zeus, god of the sky. The list of individual gods varies with the source, but the most widely accepted membership is Zeus, Hera, Poseidon, Demeter, Apollo, Artemis, Dionysus, Athena, Ares, Hephaestus, Hermes, and Aphrodite.

Primordial Four In Greek cosmogony, the Primordial Four refers to the first four known entities. According to Hesiod in his *Theogony*, the first being to come into existence was Chaos, a "vast and dark" chasm or abyss. After, but not out of, Chaos came Gaia ("earth mother"), followed by Tartarus (literally "deep place"), a cosmic prison, and finally Eros (erotic love). As well as being physical things, the Primordial Four were also considered the earliest manifestations of gods.

Titanomachy The name given to the epic, ten-year war between the Titans and the Olympian gods. After overthrowing his tyrannical father, Uranus, Cronus became fearful that he too would be overthrown by his children. He swallowed them but was tricked into letting out Zeus, who was hidden and raised on Crete. Cronus was later forced to regurgitate his other children and, together with Zeus, the Giants, and the Cyclopes (from whom Zeus received his trademark lightning bolt) battled the Titans, who were eventually defeated and cast into Tartarus.

underworld A general term used to describe the places that exist beneath the earth. The descriptions vary from one source to another, but the underworld in total included Tartarus, the cosmic prison of the Titans and the worst offending humans (particularly those, such as Tantalus and Sisyphus, who had offended the gods); Hades (or Erebus), where mortals went after death; and according to Virgil but not the Greek poets, Elysium (the Elysian Fields), the resting place of heroes. The most significant underworld river separating the living from the dead was the Styx, although it was across another river, Acheron, that Charon the ferryman carried the souls of the newly deceased.

CHAOS

the 30-second mythology

According to the early Greek

poet Hesiod, the first event to occur in the cosmos was the birth, or "coming-into-being," of Chaos. After Chaos followed Gaia (earth), Tartarus (cosmic prison), and Eros (erotic love). These beings were the Primordial Four—the first four entities identified. Everything that came into the world thereafter derived ultimately from one or more of the Primordial Four. Chaos did not signify a state of utter disorder, as the word now implies; rather it was "bounded space," as in a chasm. Indeed, the words "chaos" and "chasm" are etymologically related. In the logic of the myth Chaos offered room in which the world could develop. Chaos had a dual nature: it was not only a physical thing but also a personality, a living being out of which two other cosmic entities, Darkness and Night, emerged, which in turn produced other elements of the cosmos. Like Darkness and Night, the descendants of Chaos were mostly intangible elements such as Death, Sleep, and Discord.

3-SECOND MUSE
Hesiod's cosmogony starts midway with Chaos but does not explain what preceded Chaos or what created Chaos.

3-MINUTE ODYSSEY
In the first century CE the Roman poet Ovid presented a different mythic cosmogony, in which the world initially consisted of shapeless matter, Chaos, within which reigned confusion and discord. Opposites warred with each other: heat with cold, wet with dry, hard with soft, heavy with light. Nature or some god liberated these elements, bringing order to the universe. In Ovid's version, Chaos was truly characterized by a state of "utter disorder."

RELATED MYTH
Many cosmogonic myths tell of an initial being or substance that contains within itself many of the eventual constituents of the cosmos. Examples are Tiamat (Mesopotamia) and Ginnungagap (Scandinavia).

3-SECOND BIOGRAPHIES
GAIA
Mother earth
See page 18

URANUS
Father sky
See page 22

HADES
Realm of the dead
See page 82

TARTARUS
Cosmic prison for defeated gods and monsters
See page 86

30-SECOND TEXT
William Hansen

The first being to come into existence, Chaos is a vast and dark chasm or abyss.

EROS/CUPID

the 30-second mythology

Eros was the Greek god of sexual attraction. His Roman counterpart was Cupid. In one account Eros was one of the Primordial Four entities. He embodied the creative urge of nature. In another version he was the child of the illicit liaison between Aphrodite and Ares. In an allegorical folktale Aphrodite, jealous of the sensationally beautiful Sicilian princess Psychê, told her son Eros to prick Psychê with his arrows and cause her to love a monster. In a mix-up Eros scratched himself, causing in him a hopeless passion for the girl. Eros spirited Psychê away to his home but remained invisible. They made love. Tricked by her envious sisters, Psychê lit a lamp and saw Eros; but burned by oil in the lamp, he flew away. Attempting to imitate Psychê's success, the sisters leapt from a mountain, expecting the West Wind (Zephyr) to carry them to Eros' abode. Instead, they were dashed on the rocks. Psychê searched everywhere for Eros and was tested by impossible tasks imposed on her by Aphrodite. However, Psychê was finally reunited with her beloved Eros, who married her and made her a goddess. Together, they had a daughter, Hedonê ("pleasure"). Apuleius' *Golden Ass* contains the classic Roman version of the story.

3-SECOND MUSE
Eros is the incarnation of sexual attraction, firing arrows that strike men and women alike, causing them to desire each other.

3-MINUTE ODYSSEY
In painting and sculpture Eros is portrayed as a nude winged boy or baby armed with a bow and a quiver of arrows. In ancient painting he is present with adults when there is sexual attraction among the humans. Psychê was the deification of the human soul, portrayed in ancient mosaics as a goddess with butterfly wings (*psychê* is also Greek for "butterfly").

RELATED MYTH
Fertility gods can be either male or female, and are often paired together as in the case of Eros and Aphrodite.

3-SECOND BIOGRAPHIES
ARES/MARS
God of war, father of Eros
See page 40

APHRODITE/VENUS
Goddess of love and beauty
See page 50

30-SECOND TEXT
Barry B. Powell

Sometimes taken to be the product of an illicit affair between Aphrodite and Ares, Eros is the god of sexual desire.

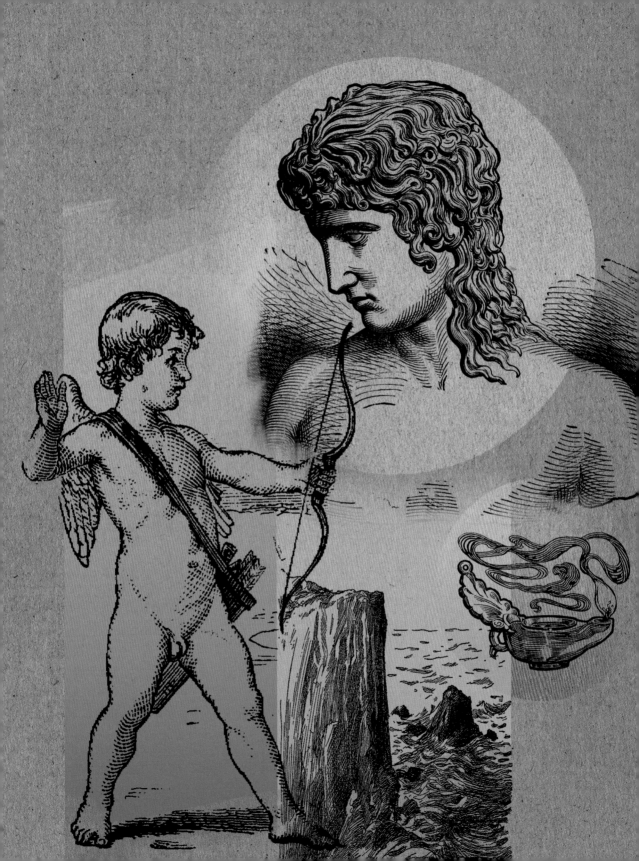

GAIA

the 30-second mythology

"Broad-bosomed earth, sure standing-place" (in the early Greek poet Hesiod's words), Gaia emerged at the very beginning of creation, after Chaos. Developing from a living entity into an outright personality, Gaia gave virgin birth to Uranus, the "sky father," then produced with him a mighty brood of children, headed by the Titans. In the strikingly Oedipal generational struggles of early Greek myth, Gaia's role is equivocal. When Uranus, fearful of his children, buried them back in her womb, Gaia gave her youngest son Cronus the adamantine sickle to castrate him; when Cronus in turn started swallowing his children, Gaia freed the youngest, Zeus, to use as a weapon against him. But when Zeus imprisoned his father, Gaia gave birth to the fearsome snaky monster Typhon to attack Zeus, only to make peace with Zeus and advise him how to counter the threat of his child Athena. Gaia's combination of the nurturing and the destructive reflected Greek male anxieties about female and maternal power. More fundamentally, Gaia was the earth itself, at once a beneficent and a ruthless mother, both womb and tomb for all the generations of earthly life.

3-SECOND MUSE
Gaia was the primordial "earth mother," the oldest of goddesses—and for many the one most powerfully still with us today.

3-MINUTE ODYSSEY
Beginning in the 1970s, the scientist James Lovelock propounded what he called (at novelist William Golding's suggestion) the "Gaia hypothesis"—the name reinforcing the concept of the earth as a single, complex, self-regulating living organism, of which human beings are a part. While scientists continue to debate Lovelock's theory, Gaia remains a powerful figure for environmental and pagan movements.

RELATED MYTH
Almost all mythologies personify the earth as a mother goddess. The Egyptians are an exception, with a male earth (Geb) and female sky (Nut).

3-SECOND BIOGRAPHIES
CHAOS
The primordial cosmic entity with which creation began
See page 14

URANUS
The "sky father," son and husband to Gaia
See page 22

THE TITANS
Children of Gaia and Uranus, the first generation of gods
See page 24

ZEUS/JUPITER
King of Olympus, god of the sky
See page 32

30-SECOND TEXT
Geoffrey Miles

Gaia is the primordial earth goddess and Zeus' grandmother.

c. 750/700 BCE
Born

c. 700/650 BCE
Composed *Theogony*

c. 700/650 BCE
Composed *Works and Days*

c. 700/650 BCE
Composed *Catalog of Women*

1493
First printed edition of *Works and Days*

1495
Complete works published in Venice

1914
Works and Days and *Theogony* translated by Hugh G. Evelyn-White

1959
Hesiod: Works and Days, Theogony, and *The Shield of Achilles* translated by Richmond Lattimore

HESIOD

Together with Homer, Hesiod is one of the two fathers of Greek poetry. Although he is the putative author of numerous works, there are two that are considered to be authentically his: *Works and Days* and the *Theogony*. Whether a single person composed these two works remains a debated issue, just as the single authorship of the *Iliad* and the *Odyssey* is still an unsettled issue. Only a little is known about Hesiod beyond what can be gleaned from internal evidence. We do know that he bemoaned the hardness and unfairness of life. Humans were at the mercy of the gods, of the physical world, and of one another.

Hesiod had inherited from his father a small patch of land at the foot of Mount Helicon, the home of the Muses. His sheep pastured on the lower slopes, and drank from one of the sacred springs—the Hippocrene.

The *Theogony* is the main source of Greek cosmogony, covering the creation, evolution, and descent of the gods and the eventual hegemony of Zeus. *Works and Days* is addressed to Hesiod's brother, Perses, with whom he had a falling out over the division of their father's estate. Where Hesiod was prudent, Perses was profligate, and asked his brother for a loan. In reply, Hesiod composed *Works and Days*, which laments the injustice of society and the hardness of life—too many mouths to feed—but which also defends the dignity of labor. *Works and Days* also describes farming techniques as well as the key myths of Prometheus and of Pandora and the Ages— the alternative myths of the loss of the equivalent of Paradise.

In contrast to Homer, who addresses kings rather than ordinary persons, Hesiod addresses fellow farmers and other commoners. Homer and Hesiod, writing independently of each other, nevertheless agree largely on the constituents of the Pantheon, though they differ on emphases and details. Together, Homer and Hesiod constitute the equivalent of the Greek Bible. Hesiod provides the myths of creation and of the fall; Homer provides subsequent human history.

URANUS

the 30-second mythology

According to Hesiod, Uranus was the son and then the husband of Gaia. He hated his offspring, pushing them down into a cranny of Gaia and thereby not allowing them to come forth. Gaia conspired with her son Cronus, a Titan, to overcome Uranus, giving Cronus an adamantine sickle (probably iron). Cronus waited in ambush from within Gaia. When Uranus came lusting for Gaia, Cronus cut off his father's genitals, which fell into the sea. The blood from the wound fell to the earth, whence sprang up the Giants ("earth-born ones"), the Erinyes (the "Furies"), and the Meliae (the ash-tree nymphs). From the foam gathered around the genitals that landed in the sea came forth Aphrodite (by false etymology, the "foam-born one"). The story attributes creation to the separation or differentiation of either gods or elements—a common mythological process. Uranus and Gaia were, in effect, locked in a perpetual embrace, allowing no place for the world to appear. Once Uranus was castrated, the Titans and the other children of Uranus and Gaia could emerge, and the creation of the world could proceed.

3-SECOND MUSE
Uranus ("sky") was a primordial Greek god who arrested the progress of the world through his tyrannous sexual demands on Gaia ("earth").

3-MINUTE ODYSSEY
Hesiod's version beckons a psychoanalytic approach. There is the incestuous relationship between Uranus and Gaia—the son who becomes husband of his own mother, and in turn the father of their children. Then there is the Oedipal-like succession of Uranus by his son Cronus, and in turn of Cronus by his son Zeus.

RELATED MYTH
In Hittite myth Kumarbi bit off the genitals of his father, Anu, the sky god, became pregnant, and (somehow) gave birth to the storm god Teshub, who deposed Kumarbi.

3-SECOND BIOGRAPHIES
CHAOS
The first primordial entity
See page 14

GAIA
Mother earth
See page 18

THE TITANS
Children of Gaia and Uranus
See page 24

30-SECOND TEXT
Barry B. Powell

Uranus, the primordial Greek sky god, is a sexual tyrant.

THE TITANS

the 30-second mythology

Gaia and Uranus gave birth to the race of Titans, who warred unsuccessfully against the Olympians in the great Titanomachy, which lasted ten years. The meaning of "Titan," in spite of many suggestions, remains unclear. In general, the Titans symbolized the powerful forces of nature, untamed by the rational and patriarchal rule of the Olympians. They were seldom represented in art and garnered little worship. Two notable Titans were the watery male Oceanus and the female Tethys, probably derived from the Babylonian watery Tiamat. Oceanus was a river that surrounded the world. According to Homer, Oceanus and Tethys gave birth to all the other gods. Oceanus also fed all the waters in wells, fountains, and rivers. From Oceanus and Tethys came the three thousand Oceanids, spirits of the sea, rivers, and springs. Other Titans include Phoebe, who may be connected with the sky, and Themis, who represented that which is fixed and settled. She controlled the Delphic Oracle before it passed to Apollo and bore children to Zeus, as did the Titan Mnemosyne, "memory." Cronus and Rhea were parents or grandparents of the Twelve Olympians, including Zeus.

3-SECOND MUSE
The Titans, whose power was awesome, were the children of Gaia and Uranus, whom the Olympians, under Zeus' leadership, defeated in a great battle.

3-MINUTE ODYSSEY
Iapetus and Themis were the parents of Prometheus, who, as the son of a Titan himself, had a long-running feud with Zeus, who had defeated and imprisoned the other Titans. In Hesiod's *Theogony* and *Works and Days* Prometheus is portrayed as a trickster, whose attempt to fool Zeus and steal fire for mankind is punished by an eagle devouring his liver.

RELATED MYTH
Similar myths about a war in heaven appear around the world—for example, the Norse wars between the Aesir and Vanir, the Babylonian war between Tiamat and Marduk, and the war between God and Satan in Christian lore.

3-SECOND BIOGRAPHIES
PROMETHEUS
Rebel god, who stole fire for mankind
See page 26

ZEUS/JUPITER
King of Olympus, god of the sky
See page 32

TARTARUS
Prison of the Titans and also the god of that prison
See page 86

30-SECOND TEXT
Barry B. Powell

The Titans, the children of Gaia and Uranus, battled the Olympians for control of the world but lost.

PROMETHEUS

the 30-second mythology

3-SECOND MUSE
Prometheus was a rebel
god who championed the
interests of humankind
against those of the ruling
Olympian gods.

3-MINUTE ODYSSEY
Prometheus combines
two roles that are found
frequently in mythologies:
culture hero and trickster.
A culture hero facilitates
human civilization by
overcoming obstacles or
by giving humans basic
information or necessities,
as when Prometheus steals
fire from the gods for
humankind. A trickster
succeeds by cunning, as
when Prometheus deceives
Zeus into choosing the pile
of bones, as a result of
which humans get a better
portion of sacrificial
victims than gods do.

In the early days of the cosmos,
the Olympian gods met with human males
to decide how meat was to be apportioned
between them. Prometheus, a son of the Titan
god Iapetus, acted as facilitator. An ox was
slaughtered, and Prometheus divided it into two
piles. One consisted of meat covered with tripe,
the other of bones covered with luscious fat.
Prometheus invited the Olympian god Zeus to
choose, and he selected the pile that looked
good but that contained mostly bones. When
Zeus perceived that he had been tricked, in
his fury he withheld fire from mankind. So
although men had meat, they could not cook it.
(According to an alternative version, Zeus knew
of the deceit but chose the inferior selection in
order to punish humans later.) But Prometheus
then stole fire from the gods and gave it to
mankind. Zeus was now doubly angry, and so
devised punishments for mankind as well as for
mankind's divine champion. For mankind he
invented womankind, ordering the craftsman
god Hephaestus to fashion from clay the first
woman, Pandora. She was foisted upon
Prometheus' slow-witted brother, Epimetheus.
As for Prometheus, Zeus had him bound to
the side of a mountain, where an eagle daily
tortured him by eating his liver.

RELATED MYTH
Culture heroes and tricksters in
myth are sometimes different
characters, sometimes a single
character. Coyote in Native
American cultures exemplifies
a character who combines
both roles.

3-SECOND BIOGRAPHIES
THE TITANS
Early family of gods
See page 24

ZEUS/JUPITER
King of the gods
See page 32

HEPHAESTUS/VULCAN
God of crafts
See page 38

HERMES/MERCURY
Messenger of the gods
See page 54

30-SECOND TEXT
William Hansen

*A wily rebel who
incurred Zeus' wrath
for stealing fire and
giving it to mankind,
Prometheus was
punished for his
impudence.*

OLYMPIANS

OLYMPIANS
GLOSSARY

aegis A broad, ceremonial collar or garment (often supporting or carrying a shield) worn to demonstrate that protection was bestowed on the wearer by a divine power. The aegis dates back to Nubian and ancient Egyptian civilizations. In Greek mythology both Zeus and Athena are each described as wearing an aegis fashioned by Hephaestus, the divine craftsman. The word is now used to mean "protection," as in, "under the aegis of the United States."

cult of Zeus The great oracle at Dodona in Epirus in northwest Greece was home to a cult of Zeus and is reputed to be the oldest oracle in Greece, dating back to the second millennium BCE. Prophecies were given by bare-footed priests, known as the Helloi or Selloi, who divined the oracles by listening to the leaves of a sacred oak tree rustling in the breeze. Priestesses later replaced the priests. The shrine at Dodona is closely associated with Dione, who in some versions is a form of "earth goddess."

Curetes Cretan mountain spirits responsible for shepherding, hunting, beekeeping, and metalwork. In Hesiod's *Theogony*, Gaia hid the child Zeus on Crete so that Cronus could not find him. She asked the Curetes to look after him—the sound of the child's cries were masked by their loud rituals. The Curetes, who worshipped Rhea, are often identified with the Phrygian Corybantes, who venerated the Phrygian counterpart Cybele.

Cyclopes The collective name for the group of one-eyed giants that appear at various times in Greek mythology. According to Hesiod's *Theogony*, the Cyclopes were one set of the children of Uranus and Gaia, who forged for Zeus the thunderbolt that was so effective in the Olympians' defeat of the Titans. The Cyclops Polyphemus, son of Poseidon, was famously tricked by Odysseus but was then avenged by his father.

Eleusinian Mysteries Sacred rituals held annually in the town of Eleusis, northwest of Athens, to honor the goddesses Persephone and Demeter. Believed to date back to the Mycenaean period, they were among the most significant ceremonies in the ancient Greek calendar and were a combination of secret initiation and celebration with, at their heart, the concept of death and rebirth. The festivities are believed to have lasted for around nine days during September, and were also closely associated with the sowing of crops—with Demeter as the goddess of grain and fertility.

mermen The male counterparts to mermaids. They were portrayed as bearded, with green hair, and carrying a trident. They had a human head, arms, and torso, but a fishlike tail instead of legs. The two most famous mermen in Greek mythology were Triton, the son of Poseidon, and Glaucus, a once mortal fisherman who was transformed into a merman after eating a magical plant.

omnipotent Although the gods in classical mythology were powerful, none of them were omnipotent, or all-powerful. Even Zeus was challenged by other gods, of whom he was often fearful, and unable to override Fate. The term is more accurately reserved for monotheistic religions. Yet even religions with a single god do not always deem that god to be omnipotent, which tends to be a philosophical rather than popular concept.

parthenogenesis (literally "virgin birth") A form of asexual reproduction, and a common means of reproduction in the animal world, parthenogenesis was often found in classical mythology. Many of the key goddesses, from the primordial Gaia to Hera, wife and sister of Zeus, are capable of reproducing without sexual intercourse. The birth of Athena out of Zeus' head was not parthenogenetic since Athena had already been conceived with the goddess Metis. The term is also used to describe Jesus' birth.

psychopomp Name given to an entity that guides newly deceased souls to the next world or afterlife. There are numerous examples of psychopomps in classical mythology, notably Charon, Hermes, Hecate, and Morpheus.

trident A large three-pronged spear associated with Poseidon (Neptune). Poseidon used his trident in a variety of ways, but primarily to create sources of water, to cause earthquakes, and to conjure up storms. Mermen are also often depicted as carrying tridents.

ZEUS/JUPITER

the 30-second mythology

As well as the god of the sky,
Zeus was also the god of social customs—the
protector of kings and of strangers. The Roman
Jupiter was, even more, the embodiment of the
state and its irresistible military power. Zeus
was the youngest child of Cronus and Rhea.
He was married to Hera, though he is famous
for his amorous adventures that resulted in
many offspring. Cronus sired children by his
wife Rhea, but, like his father before him, he
was a tyrant, swallowing the children as soon
as they were born. When Zeus, Rhea's last
child, was born, she instead gave Cronus a
stone wrapped in swaddling clothes, which he
unwittingly swallowed. Rhea secretly took the
infant Zeus to Crete, where he was raised in a
cave. Followers called Curetes beat their shields
outside the cave to hide the infant's crying.
When Zeus grew up, he overthrew Cronus and
forced him to vomit up the children he had
swallowed. There followed the Titanomachy,
or battle against the Titans, in which, thanks
to the thunderbolt manufactured by the
Cyclopes, Zeus and the Olympians were
victorious. Despite his supremacy Zeus was
not omnipotent. He was challenged by other
gods and was subject to Fate.

3-SECOND MUSE
Zeus (or Jupiter to the
Romans) was the king
of the gods, the head of
the Olympian family—the
"father of gods and men,"
as Homer put it.

3-MINUTE ODYSSEY
At Dodona in Epirus,
in remote northwest
Greece, was a cult of Zeus
centered on a sacred oak.
There priestesses gave
prophecies by listening to
the rustling of the leaves
of the oak tree. At Dodona
Zeus' consort was Dione,
a feminine form of Zeus,
not Hera. Dione may have
been Zeus' original consort
before the Greeks arrived
in the Balkan peninsula
and took over a local cult
of the mother goddess
(that is, Hera).

RELATED MYTH
In Sanskrit there is a god Dyaus
Pita, "father Zeus," who is
like the Greek/Roman god. In
Norse myth the name of the
god Tyr ("Tuesday") is based on
the same Indo-European root.

3-SECOND BIOGRAPHIES
URANUS/SATURN
Father of the Olympians
See page 22

HERA/JUNO
Queen of the gods,
wife of Zeus/Jupiter
See page 34

30-SECOND TEXT
Barry B. Powell

*The youngest child
of Cronus and Rhea,
Zeus is the king of the
gods and leads them
to victory against the
Titans. A prodigious
lover, he fathers many
gods and heroes.*

HERA/JUNO
the 30-second mythology

As one of the children of Cronus, the former ruler of the universe, Hera was never likely to be satisfied with second place, yet she played second-fiddle as the wife of her brother Zeus. She was, however, hardly a subservient wife, except on those occasions when Zeus was able to coerce her into submission with threats of domestic violence. And well she might have been frightened: her husband had once hung her from the summit of Olympus by her wrists with her feet weighted down by anvils. Most often, however, her anger was directed at the various lovers and illegitimate children of Zeus rather than at the god himself. Heracles, the greatest of Zeus' mortal offspring, was the most persistently persecuted until he died. After he was made immortal, Hera gave him her daughter Hebe as wife. Unlike her husband, she took no lovers. At the same time she was capable of having children without him. Her response to his production of Athena out of his own head, though only after intercourse with the goddess Metis, was to give birth to Hephaestus by parthenogenesis ("maiden-birth"), that is, entirely by herself. In a Roman take on this story, after Minerva appeared out of Jupiter's head, Flora gave Juno a magical herb to impregnate her with Mars.

3-SECOND MUSE
Hera, linked by the Romans with their marriage goddess Juno, was both Zeus' sister and queen.

3-MINUTE ODYSSEY
Zeus and Hera were hardly considered an old married couple even though their marriage was made around the time of Zeus' rise to supremacy. This was because, after bathing annually at a sacred spring in Argos, Hera would renew her virginity and celebrate her marriage all over again. An ancient "every woman," she was revered in Stymphalos as virgin, wife, and—interestingly, in view of the immortal status of her husband—widow.

RELATED MYTH
As the Queen of Olympus, Hera shared some traits of the Phoenician great goddess Astarte, and of the Mesopotamian Ishtar.

3-SECOND BIOGRAPHIES
ZEUS/JUPITER
King of Olympus, god of the sky
See page 32

HEPHAESTUS/VULCAN
God of crafts, blacksmith to the gods
See page 38

ARES/MARS
God of war, son of Zeus and Hera
See page 40

HERACLES/HERCULES
Greek hero of immense strength
See page 96

30-SECOND TEXT
Susan Deacy

Hera is locked in a conflict-ridden marriage with Zeus, whose infidelities fuel repeated acts of vindictive persecution.

POSEIDON/NEPTUNE
the 30-second mythology

Together with his brothers, Zeus and Hades, Poseidon cast lots for sovereignty over the world. Zeus took the sky, Hades the underworld, and Poseidon the sea. Poseidon's emblem was the trident, a three-pronged spear with which he could strike the ground, causing springs to emerge. His most significant consort, of whom there were many, was the sea nymph Amphitrite, and together they had a merman son, Triton. When Poseidon and Athena competed for sponsorship of the city of Athens, Poseidon struck the Acropolis with his trident, and a salt spring burst forth. Athena, however, planted an olive tree and was chosen by the Athenians as their civic deity. In revenge, Poseidon flooded the plain of Attica, on which Athens stands. Poseidon was the father of Theseus and of many other heroes, but some of his children were more than human. In one myth Poseidon courted the goddess Demeter, but his love was not reciprocated. To avoid him she turned herself into a mare. Poseidon, however, became a stallion and covered her; their offspring was the magical horse Arion. Unlike other primordial water gods, Poseidon is a fully-fledged personality, and one separate from the natural phenomenon he controls.

3-SECOND MUSE
Son of the Titans Cronus and Rhea, Poseidon—identified with the Roman god Neptune—was the powerful god of the sea, earthquake, and horses.

3-MINUTE ODYSSEY
In punishment for a disagreement, Zeus forced Poseidon and Apollo to serve King Laomedon of Troy. Laomedon ordered them to build Troy's massive walls but then refused to pay them as he had promised. To punish the Trojans, Poseidon sent a great sea monster against the city. Heracles killed it in return for Laomedon's daughter. Poseidon was the divine enemy of Odysseus because he blinded his son, the Cyclops Polyphemus. Poseidon delayed Odysseus' return home to Ithaca for ten years.

RELATED MYTH
Other mythological water gods are the Egyptian Nun and the Babylonian Tiamat.

3-SECOND BIOGRAPHIES
POLYPHEMUS
The Cyclops son of Poseidon
See page 68

ODYSSEUS/ULYSSES
King of Ithaca whose Trojan Horse led to Troy's downfall
See page 102

THESEUS
Hero of Athens, son of Poseidon
See page 106

30-SECOND TEXT
Barry B. Powell

The god of the sea, like his brother Zeus, engages in numerous sexual conquests. Poseidon's emblem is the trident.

HEPHAESTUS/ VULCAN

the 30-second mythology

Hephaestus was depicted as

either the son of Zeus and Hera, or of Hera alone. In this version, his mother conceived him spontaneously to take revenge on her husband when he gave birth to Athena. That it is Hephaestus who in some versions facilitates the birth of Athena provides a further instance of mythological flexibility, as does the question of how Hephaestus became lame. Either Hera's horror at producing a disabled child led her to hurl him off Olympus, or it was the fall that caused the disability. Hephaestus' lameness marginalized him on Olympus, however much his fellow deities needed the gifts that he was uniquely qualified to provide. As well as equipping the gods with their various weapons and other attributes, he helped particular Olympians to get out of certain tricky situations. When, for example, Athena was stuck, fully developed, inside the head of Zeus, it was the ax blow of Hephaestus that released her. His skill at craft also enabled him to turn particular situations to his favor, as when his unfaithful wife, Aphrodite, found herself caught with her lover Ares in a net so fine that it looked invisible.

3-SECOND MUSE
Hephaestus—identified with the Roman god Vulcan—was the divine craftsman, whose talent at fashioning intricate objects was regarded as unrivaled.

3-MINUTE ODYSSEY
As well as creating such wondrous, not to mention indestructible, objects as Athena's aegis, Aphrodite's girdle, and the armor of Achilles, Hephaestus was also responsible for creations that were so cleverly constructed that they appeared to be alive. He was also key to the creation of specific human beings, including Pandora—the first woman—and Erichthonius, through whom Athenians could claim the status of "children of Hephaestus."

RELATED MYTH
Hephaestus shares traits with several clever gods often known as "tricksters," for example, Enki of the Sumerians and a range of Native American figures.

3-SECOND BIOGRAPHIES
ZEUS/JUPITER
King of Olympus, god of the sky
See page 32

HERA/JUNO
Queen of the gods, wife of Zeus/Jupiter
See page 34

APHRODITE/VENUS
Goddess of love and beauty
See page 50

ATHENA/MINERVA
Goddess of wisdom, warfare, and justice
See page 52

30-SECOND TEXT
Susan Deacy

Known for his skill, craftsmanship, and ingenuity the lame Hephaestus is married to the goddess of love, Aphrodite.

ARES/MARS

the 30-second mythology

The name for the Roman god

Mars may derive from the same root as Ares, the Greek god of war, but Mars represented heroic valor while Ares represented the violence and bloodlust of war. Ares was thus very different from Athena, who espoused military intelligence and strategic thinking. Outright opposite to Ares was Aphrodite, the goddess of love. Yet the two became lovers, even though she was married to the crippled god Hephaestus, whom she despised. The sun god Helios, who sees all, informed Hephaestus of the affair, and so the craftsman god contrived a trap of a fine golden mesh suspended over the wedding bed. He told his wife that he was going to Lemnos, but he soon returned to catch Ares in bed with Aphrodite. He sprang the trap, and the net imprisoned the naked gods. All the other Olympians came to look and sneer, but the goddesses held back for modesty. At last the lovers were freed. Ares went to Thrace, his homeland, and Aphrodite went to Paphos in Cyprus, the site of her birth. Deimos ("terror") and Phobos ("fear") were the offspring of Ares and Aphrodite, and today give their names to two moons of the planet Mars.

3-SECOND MUSE
One of the Olympians, Ares ("battle" or "curse") was the god not merely of war but of slaughter and bloodlust, in which he delighted.

3-MINUTE ODYSSEY
Ares took the side of Troy in the epic Trojan War. Yet despite all his power, such as when entering the body of Hector and forcing back the Greek lines almost single-handedly, he was not able to secure victory for the Trojans. In his book *Civilization and its Discontents*, Freud sees love and war (aggression) as the key drives in humans, and sees them as opposed, just as Aphrodite and Ares are.

RELATED MYTH
The Norse god Tyr, the god of war, was akin to Ares. From the name Tyr comes our "Tuesday." He was, however, surpassed in fighting by Odin, or Wotan, the chief of the Norse gods and one compared with Zeus. From the name Wotan comes our "Wednesday."

3-SECOND BIOGRAPHIES
HEPHAESTUS/VULCAN
God of craftsmen
See page 38

APHRODITE/VENUS
Goddess of love and beauty
See page 50

30-SECOND TEXT
Barry B. Powell

Ares' lust for battle stands opposite to Aphrodite's devotion to love and beauty, yet the two were lovers.

APOLLO

the 30-second mythology

The ever youthful Apollo was

the son of Zeus and Leto, and was the twin brother of Artemis. Before being integrated into the Olympian family, Apollo was feared by the regions of the earth and by the gods. Only Delos—a floating island that could claim not to be, strictly, a "land"—was willing to host his birth. Seeming to bear out a prophecy that he would "greatly lord it among gods and mortal men" (*Homeric Hymn to Apollo* 68–9), Apollo, upon arriving at the house of Zeus, stretched his bow. In fear, the other gods left their thrones till Leto disarmed him. Apollo's achievements included his victory over the serpent Python, the previous ruler of Delphi. The site thereafter became his foremost place of worship. In response to slights upon his mother's honor, Apollo took joint vengeance with his twin and fellow archer, Artemis. When Niobe boasted that she was more fertile than Leto, the pair shot and killed her children. Among his other deeds were ones for which he incurred punishment. For slaying the Cyclopes, for instance, Zeus made him spend a year tending the livestock of the mortal Admetus.

3-SECOND MUSE
Apollo, who came to be identified with the sun god Helios, was the patron of many things, including poetry, prophecy, music, medicine, and plagues.

3-MINUTE ODYSSEY
Apollo preached, but did not always practice, moderation in life. On several occasions, his attempts to deflower females failed. For example, Cassandra retained her virginity as did her fellow prophetess, the Sibyl of Cumae; meanwhile, Daphne escaped rape through transformation into a laurel. These failures notwithstanding, Apollo was the father of several children, including the healing god Asclepius (by Coronis), the herdsman Aristaeus (by Cyrene), and Ion, the product of his rape of Creusa.

RELATED MYTH
The Near Eastern god who bears closest similarity to Apollo is the Hurrian plague deity, Aplu.

3-SECOND BIOGRAPHY
ZEUS/JUPITER
King of Olympus, god of the sky
See page 32

30-SECOND TEXT
Susan Deacy

This god of music, good health, and the sun was at the same time a vengeance-seeking, plague-bringing god, some of whose beloveds, like his enemies, came to unfortunate ends.

Eighth century BCE
Homer active?

750 BCE
The *Iliad*, then *Odyssey*
composed—both prior
to Hesiod

Second century BCE
"Stabilized" text of
both poems composed
in Alexandria

15th century
Homer rediscovered in
Renaissance Italy

1488
The first printed edition
of the *Iliad* and the
Odyssey

1675–1676
Thomas Hobbes'
translation of both works
published

1700
John Dryden's version
of the *Iliad* published

1898–1900
The *Iliad* and the
Odyssey translated by
Samuel Butler

1961
The *Iliad* translated by
Richard Lattimore

1989
The *Iliad* translated by
Robert Fitzgerald

1998
The *Odyssey* translated
by Robert Fitzgerald

HOMER

Although he is among the best-known ancient Greek poets and the author of two of the most influential epic poems in Western literature—the *Iliad* and the *Odyssey* —little is known about Homer. He might have been born on the island of Chios, or at Smyrna on the coast of Turkey. There was an ancient tradition that he was blind (in some dialects the word *omeros* is associated with blindness). Herodotus was insistent that Homer predated him by some 400 years, which puts Homer at around 850 BCE. Others maintain that Homer was an eyewitness (blind or sighted) to the Trojan War and therefore must have lived in the 12th century BCE. A third possibility is that there was more than one Homer, just as there might have been more than one Hesiod. The ancients almost uniformly assumed a single Homer, and the suggestion of multiple authors became popular only as part of the rise of modern critical approaches to ancient texts of all kinds. The problems of the authorship of more than one work are common, such as with the many letters attributed to St. Paul. One of Homer's famous translators, Samuel Butler, argued that Homer might have been a woman.

While scholars in the 20th century came mostly to return to the ancient view of a single Homer, everyone grants that the two works present differing views of the relations among the gods and of the relations between gods and humans. Still, both works assume a common view of the place of the gods and of Fate in human affairs. Both works emphasize the unhappy nature of life after death in Hades. At the same time both works stress the need for the burial of the dead. Above all, both works, though especially the *Iliad*, are about aristocrats and not about ordinary Greeks or Trojans.

Both epics, like other ancient works, were originally oral and were written down only later. Some scholars maintain that the works were standardized in the eighth century BCE, others that they became standardized in the seventh century BCE and were written down in the sixth century. The Greek alphabet was established in the eighth century BCE, so, that the poems could not have been written down any earlier. Doubtless the *Iliad*, which is about the origin and the last year of the Trojan War, was composed earlier than the *Odyssey*, which is about Odysseus' return home following the end of the war. But who Homer was and, even now, how many Homers there were are still debated by classicists.

ARTEMIS/DIANA

the 30-second mythology

Artemis, identified by the

Romans with Diana, was the very dangerous goddess of the hunt, wild animals, wilderness, and later the moon. She was responsible for the mysterious deaths of women. Her parents were Zeus and the nymph Leto, and she is often shown with her bow and arrows and her twin brother Apollo, who was her constant companion. Hera, furious at Zeus' infidelity with Leto, commanded that she could give birth on no place "that saw the light of day." Delos, at the center of the Cyclades, was a floating island, bobbing beneath the surface. There the suffering Leto gave birth to Artemis, who then immediately helped to deliver her brother. She was thus recognized as protecting women in childbirth. When Artemis was bathing, the hunter Actaeon saw her naked. Offended and ashamed, she transformed him into a stag. Actaeon's own dogs, not recognizing their master, tore him to pieces. Niobe thought she was better than Leto because she had seven boys and seven girls, whereas Leto gave birth only to Artemis and Apollo. In response, Apollo killed her sons with his arrows, and Artemis shot her daughters. Devastated, Niobe turned into a stone that even now is said to weep in the mountains of western Turkey.

3-SECOND MUSE

Artemis was the virgin goddess of the forest, known to Homer as *potnia Thêrôn*, "mistress of the wild animals." She presided over the hunt, childbirth, and the sudden death of women.

3-MINUTE ODYSSEY

Artemis was an ally of the Trojans. When the Greek King Agamemnon killed a stag in her sacred grove and then boasted that he was a better hunter than Artemis, she required the sacrificial death of his daughter Iphigenia before she would allow the winds to take the Greeks to Troy. According to one version, at the last minute she substituted a deer for the girl, whom she carried to the Crimea to serve as her priestess.

RELATED MYTH

The Thracian goddess Bendis, also a goddess of the moon and hunting, is closely associated with Artemis and Diana.

3-SECOND BIOGRAPHIES

APOLLO
God of prophecy and the sun
See page 42

ACTAEON
Hunter who saw Artemis naked
See page 134

30-SECOND TEXT

Barry B. Powell

Artemis is Apollo's sister and the goddess of hunting. Unlike most Olympians, she is strictly chaste.

DEMETER/CERES
the 30-second mythology

The daughter of Cronus and Rhea, Demeter (meaning "earth mother") was one of the earliest Olympians. She oversaw the growth of crops and all aspects of fertility, including childbirth. Her daughter, Persephone (Roman Proserpina), was abducted by Hades and became queen of the underworld. Grief-stricken, Demeter stopped all growth across the earth. As she searched for her daughter, she disguised herself as an old woman. She spent some time in Eleusis, where, in gratitude, she tried to bestow immortality on the king's infant son, Demophon—an effort that backfired. She continued her search until she discovered Persephone's whereabouts and demanded her release. As a compromise, Zeus allowed Persephone to spend part of the year with Demeter and part with Hades, providing a mythological reason for the changing seasons. In a more sublime sense, Demeter and Persephone were worshipped in the Eleusinian Mysteries (secret initiation ceremonies) as goddesses who eased the transition between life and death. Although she was generally seen as a benevolent figure, she could be dangerous if insulted. When Erysichthon cut down trees in her sacred grove, Demeter punished him with an insatiable craving for food. He ate and ate but remained insatiable.

3-SECOND MUSE
Demeter, known to the Romans as "Ceres," was goddess of the harvest and fertility, and was seen as a second goddess of the earth itself.

3-MINUTE ODYSSEY
Demeter was unlucky in love. She gave birth to Persephone after sleeping with Zeus, but when Demeter fell in love with Iasion and bore him a son, Ploutos, Zeus killed Iasion out of jealousy. Demeter's problems continued while searching for Persephone. She was pursued by her brother Poseidon, and when she was transformed into a horse to escape, Poseidon changed into a stallion. The ensuing liaison resulted in the birth of an immortal horse, Arion.

RELATED MYTH
Adonis was also fought over by gods—specifically goddesses—and joint custody had to be granted by Zeus. Primordial mother figures are found in many mythologies, from the Egyptian Isis to the Inuit Aakuluujjusi.

3-SECOND BIOGRAPHIES
ZEUS/JUPITER
King of Olympus, god of the sky
See page 32

POSEIDON/NEPTUNE
God of the sea and of horses
See page 36

DIONYSUS/BACCHUS
God of wine, son of Zeus
See page 56

HADES
The underworld, and the name given to its king
See page 82

30-SECOND TEXT
Emma Griffiths

Demeter is an earth mother, whose annual separation from her daughter is supposed to explain the changing seasons.

APHRODITE/VENUS

the 30-second mythology

Aphrodite means "born of foam" (from the Greek *aphros*). She was created when the Titan Cronus threw the mutilated genitals of his father, Uranus, into the sea, where they foamed and boiled, and out of which, on the shores of Cyprus, appeared Aphrodite—a beautiful, young woman, carried on a scallop shell. An alternative version maintains that she was the daughter of Zeus and Dione, an avatar of the earth goddess. Aphrodite can be taken as either the source or the manifestation of the overwhelming and often destructive power of love. Realizing that her beauty would bring trouble, Zeus married her to the ugly and crippled Hephaestus, who, rather counterproductively, created for her a magical, jeweled girdle that made her even more irresistible. Aphrodite had affairs with gods and mortals indiscriminately. She enjoyed liaisons with the mortal Trojan prince Anchises, resulting in the birth of Aeneas, and with the god Hermes, resulting in the birth of Hermaphroditus. She also had a long dalliance with Adonis. Her longest affair was with Ares (Mars), out of which she gave birth to Eros, the armed god of sexual desire whose indiscriminate arrows explain or express the capriciousness and painfulness of love.

RELATED MYTH
Parallel to Aphrodite are the goddesses Astarte (Phoenician), Hathor (Egyptian), Inanna (Babylonian), Ishtar (Akkadian), and Freya (Norse).

3-SECOND BIOGRAPHIES
ZEUS/JUPITER
King of Olympus, god of the sky
See page 32

HERA/JUNO
Queen of Olympus, consort to Zeus
See page 34

HEPHAESTUS/VULCAN
God of crafts, blacksmith to the gods
See page 38

ARES/MARS
God of war, son of Zeus and Hera
See page 40

30-SECOND TEXT
Viv Croot

The goddess of beauty, pleasure, love, and procreation beguiles gods and mortals alike.

ATHENA/MINERVA
the 30-second mythology

Athena was born as a by-product of Zeus' attempt to retain his throne after hearing that the son born to his first wife, Metis, would unseat him. His response was to swallow Metis, who was pregnant with Athena at the time. The child remained stuck inside Zeus until an ax-wielding Hephaestus or, in some versions, Prometheus struck open his head and the fully-grown Athena leapt out, wearing flashing armor, to the astonishment of the assembled gods. Cosmic chaos ensued until, by removing her weapons, Athena restored normality. Athena took possession of her favorite city, Athens, when her gift of the first olive tree was preferred to the salt spring created by her rival, Poseidon. Her tie to Athens was strengthened through her involvement in the birth of Erichthonius, one of its ancestral heroes. When she went to Hephaestus to ask him to make weapons, he attempted to rape her. During their struggle Hephaestus' semen fell to the ground and a child, Erichthonius ("very-earthy"), emerged from the fertilized earth. Gaia, the earth goddess, handed the child to Athena, who then reared him. Athena was credited with numerous inventions, including the flute, the ship, the horse-bit, the plow, and the chariot.

3-SECOND MUSE
Athena—identified with the Roman goddess Minerva—was at once a warrior-maiden, city-protectress, mother, craftsperson, helper of heroes, and inventor.

3-MINUTE ODYSSEY
Athena was the patron of so many heroes that one might say that one of the qualifications for heroism was to have her on one's side. An array of males—including Heracles, Perseus, Odysseus, and Jason—flourished under her protection. Her wrath was equally effective, as the Greeks discovered when, after the sack of Troy, they failed to punish the lesser Ajax for the rape of Cassandra at Athena's sacred image, the Palladium.

RELATED MYTH
Athena is akin to other warrior goddesses, including the Hittite sun goddess of Arinna and the Hindu deity Durga.

3-SECOND BIOGRAPHIES

ZEUS/JUPITER
King of Olympus, god of the sky
See page 32

HERACLES/HERCULES
Greek hero of immense strength
See page 96

ODYSSEUS/ULYSSES
Greek hero whose Trojan Horse defeated Troy
See page 102

PERSEUS
Greek hero who killed Medusa
See page 108

30-SECOND TEXT
Susan Deacy

The warrior-maiden Athena is the patron of numerous cities and many heroes.

HERMES/MERCURY
the 30-second mythology

3-SECOND MUSE
Hermes was the
light-footed, light-
fingered, and smooth-
tongued messenger of
the gods, known to
Romans as Mercury.

3-MINUTE ODYSSEY
The Homeric Hymn to
Hermes celebrates the god
as child prodigy. When he
was only one day old, he
leapt from his cradle and
stole a herd of cattle
from his half-brother
Apollo, who remained
unconvinced by Hermes'
protestations that he was
only an innocent baby.
But Hermes pacified
Apollo by the gift of a
musical instrument that he
had just invented out of a
tortoise shell—the lyre.

As shining, slippery, and mercurial
as the liquid metal to which he gave his (Roman)
name, Hermes was the messenger of the gods.
Flying between Olympus and earth on the wings
of his broad-brimmed hat and sandals, and
carrying his snake-entwined herald's rod (the
caduceus), he took messages to mortals from
his father, Zeus. Sometimes he brought help,
as when he showed Odysseus the magic herb
that saved him from Circe's enchantment.
Other times he brought stern divine commands,
as when he told Aeneas to leave Dido and
establish the future site of Rome. Talker, trader,
traveler, trickster, and thief, Hermes presided
over all forms of exchange and communication.
His skill with words made him the patron of
writers and orators, of academics and diplomats.
He saw to the circulation of goods by
merchants and thieves (not that dissimilar, in
the ancient Greeks' view), and watched over
travelers and border crossers. As he himself
crossed the boundary between heaven and
earth, he also crossed the one between life
and death. As psychopomp, or spirit guide, he
conducted the souls of the dead to Hades—and,
very occasionally, back again. In the Hellenistic
period Hermes became associated with wisdom,
hence the term "hermeneutics": the study of
the principles of interpretation.

RELATED MYTH
Hermes and the Egyptian
god Thoth are combined in
the figure of the wise Hermes
Trismegistus. The Celtic
Ogmios is a god of eloquence
and is also a psychopomp.

3-SECOND BIOGRAPHIES
ZEUS/JUPITER
King of Olympus, god
of the sky
See page 32

APOLLO
God of light, music, and poetry
See page 42

HADES
The name of both the
underworld and its king
See page 82

ODYSSEUS/ULYSSES
Greek warrior, traveler,
and trickster
See page 102

30-SECOND TEXT
Geoffrey Miles

*More than simply
a messenger, Zeus'
fleet-footed son
is the original
"mercurial" genius.*

DIONYSUS/BACCHUS
the 30-second mythology

A figure connected with both physical and social phenomena, Dionysus was associated with wine, ecstasy, communality, mystery cult, and death. Classical Dionysiac myths communicate the joys of a god who, according to one epithet, was the "Liberator" (Eleutherios). Under his power, women rushed to the mountainside, and men practiced hedonism. The various disastrous attempts to resist Dionysus are illustrated by the punishment meted out to Pentheus, Dionysus' cousin, who was torn apart by his mother and aunts. Meanwhile the daughters of Minyas, who remained at their looms after their fellow Boeotian women had dashed off to the mountainside in bacchic frenzy, came themselves to be so thoroughly inspired by Dionysian madness that, in some versions, they tore apart one of their own children. Distraught, they roamed the mountain until Hermes transformed them into bats. As the "twice born" god, Dionysus was torn from the womb of Semele as she was being incinerated by Zeus' lightning. The fetus was sewn into the thigh of Zeus, out of which the god was eventually born. He was born yet again after the Titans dismembered him, Athena producing a reconstructed Dionysus from the still-beating heart.

3-SECOND MUSE
Dionysus, the "most terrible, and most gentle, to humankind," has survived more fully as a symbol of one side of human nature than have most other ancient gods.

3-MINUTE ODYSSEY
In the 19th century stories of Dionysus' arrival from the East were thought to explain away why the Greeks worshipped a deity supposedly at odds with the rationality for which they were famed. Since the discovery of a being named DI-WO-NI-SO-JO on the Mycenaean Greek Linear B tablets, it has become clear his worship goes back at least to the Bronze Age.

RELATED MYTH
Dionysus' mixed parentage, his connections with wine and mystery, and his death and rebirth all led to the suggestion of parallels to the life of Jesus.

3-SECOND BIOGRAPHIES
THE TITANS
Children of Gaia and Uranus
See page 24

ZEUS/JUPITER
King of Olympus, god of the sky
See page 32

HEPHAESTUS/VULCAN
God of crafts, blacksmith to the gods
See page 38

ATHENA/MINERVA
Goddess of wisdom, warfare, and justice
See page 52

30-SECOND TEXT
Susan Deacy

From wine to ecstasy to death, Dionysus' array of responsibilities may explain his enduring appeal.

MONSTERS

aegis A broad, ceremonial collar or garment (often supporting or carrying a shield) worn to demonstrate that protection was bestowed on the wearer by a divine power. The aegis dates back to Nubian and ancient Egyptian civilizations. In Greek mythology both Zeus and Athena are each described as wearing an aegis fashioned by Hephaestus, the divine craftsman. The word is now used to mean "protection," as in, "under the aegis of the United States."

Argonauts Named after the ship in which they sailed, the *Argo*, the Argonauts were a group of heroic adventurers who joined Jason on his voyage to Colchis on the shores of the Black Sea in search of the Golden Fleece. The number of Argonauts varies from source to source, but around 50 is the most common figure, and among them were some of the most famous ancient heroes, notably Heracles, Orpheus, and Theseus.

Chimaera Greek mythological monster that had the body of a lioness, a tail that ended with a snake's head, and a goat's neck and head emerging from its back. Capable of breathing fire, the monster was usually portrayed as female. According to Hesiod, she was the offspring of Echidna.

Cyclopes The collective name given to the group of one-eyed giants that appear at various times in Greek mythology. According to Hesiod in the *Theogony*, the Cyclopes were three primordial sons of Uranus and Gaia who forged for Zeus the thunderbolt that was so decisive in the Olympians' defeat of the Titans. The best-known Cyclops was Polyphemus, the son of Poseidon, who was famously tricked by Odysseus.

labyrinth In Greek mythology, an extraordinarily complex construction of corridors. It was designed by Daedalus on behalf of King Minos of Crete and was built to imprison the Minotaur, a man with a bull's head. The location of the labyrinth is not known, although there are some who believe that it may have been on the site of the Knossos palace complex, a theory that was inspired by travelers' reports describing the intricate layout of the palace.

metamorphosis The transformation of one object into another; in mythology usually a human into an animal or plant. Ancient Greek mythology is full of examples of metamorphoses, often either undertaken deliberately by a god or goddess in order to fulfill a personal quest or ambition, such as Zeus turning himself into a swan in order to seduce Leda, or enacted on a mortal by a god or goddess as a form of punishment, as when Artemis turned Actaeon into a stag. It has been suggested that the myths of metamorphoses in early religions served to explain the transformation from one species to another.

underworld A general term used to describe the place that exists beneath the earth. The descriptions and realms are fluid from one source to another, but the underworld often comprised Tartarus, the cosmic prison of the Titans and of the worst human offenders; Hades (or Erebus), where mortals went after death; and Elysium (the Elysian Fields), the resting place of heroes. The most significant underworld river separating the living from the dead was the Styx, although it was across another river, Acheron, that Charon the ferryman carried the souls of the newly deceased.

THE MINOTAUR

the 30-second mythology

The Minotaur, rarely remembered by his name Asterion (the "starry one"), was the result of King Minos' hubris. In the grip of a fraternal power struggle for the throne of Crete, Minos appealed to Poseidon. The god sent him a white bull from the sea, which Minos was to sacrifice. It was such a splendid beast that the king kept it for himself and sacrificed a lesser animal instead. In revenge, Poseidon asked Aphrodite to make Minos' wife, Pasiphae, fall hopelessly in love with the bull, which she did. She then commanded Daedalus to build a wooden cow into which she could climb to consummate her passion. She suckled the resultant bull-headed child, the Minotaur, but when it became too wild and aggressive, Minos ordered Daedalus to build the labyrinth to imprison it. Through political machinations, Minos was able to demand tribute from Aegeus, King of Athens, in the form of a supply of maidens and youths to feed the Minotaur. After three years, the Athenian hero Theseus volunteered to be part of the tribute. With the help of Ariadne, Minos' daughter, and a ball of twine to mark the route, he fought and killed the Minotaur, cut off its head, and escaped from the labyrinth.

3-SECOND MUSE
With the body of a man and the head of a bull, the Minotaur was the offspring of Pasiphae, wife of Minos of Crete, and a white bull.

3-MINUTE ODYSSEY
Minos/Minotaur is sometimes taken as the embodiment of the Cretan sun god, who is usually depicted as a bull. Crete has always been associated with bulls. When Zeus fell in love with the Phoenician princess Europa, he disguised himself as a white bull, lured her onto his back, and then swam off with her to Crete.

RELATED MYTH
In Japanese classical literature the ushi-oni is a bull-headed demon. It takes various forms but is typically a horned and ferocious monster.

3-SECOND BIOGRAPHIES
POSEIDON/NEPTUNE
God of the sea and horses, brother to Zeus
See page 36

APHRODITE/VENUS
Goddess of love and beauty
See page 50

THESEUS
Founding King of Athens
See page 106

30-SECOND TEXT
Viv Croot

The Minotaur, appeased only by sacrifice, caused terror and dread until it was slain by Theseus.

MEDUSA & THE GORGONS

the 30-second mythology

3-SECOND MUSE
Medusa was originally a beautiful woman who was transformed into one of the three Gorgons—the ugliest and most terrifying monsters of the classical world.

3-MINUTE ODYSSEY
Perseus was not just Medusa's slayer but her midwife as well. All the time she was a monster, she was pregnant with her children by Poseidon. These children—the warrior Chrysoar and the winged horse, Pegasus—could not be released until Perseus had cut off her head. After various adventures with the head, Perseus presented it to Athena, who put it on her aegis.

Medusa's story began when
she slept with Poseidon in a "forbidden" place, which was either a temple of Athena or a flower meadow—a place where seduction frequently took place in mythology. For this sexual transgression, Athena turned Medusa from a beautiful-haired, young woman into a serpent-haired monster with boar's tusks, a beard, a protruding tongue, wings, and a gaze so horrible that it could turn onlookers to stone. But Athena's wrath did not end with this metamorphosis. When Perseus accepted the quest for the head of the Gorgon, Athena helped him decapitate the sleeping monster. Medusa, who was mortal, had two immortal sisters, who shared her monstrous appearance. These were Steno ("mighty") and Euryale ("far-leaping"). Along with Medusa ("cunning"), these daughters of the primordial sea gods, Phorcys and Ceto, were depicted as dwelling at the extreme end of the world, beside the streams of Ocean.

RELATED MYTH
The lolling tongue in descriptions of the Hindu goddess Kali is like the protruding tongue of the Gorgons.

3-SECOND BIOGRAPHIES
POSEIDON/NEPTUNE
God of the sea and horses, brother to Zeus
See page 36

ATHENA/MINERVA
Goddess of wisdom, warfare, and justice
See page 52

PERSEUS
Greek hero who killed Medusa
See page 108

30-SECOND TEXT
Susan Deacy

Once a beautiful woman, Medusa offends the goddess Athena, who turns her into a hideous, snake-headed Gorgon.

CERBERUS

the 30-second mythology

Cerberus had an impressive

pedigree. He was the offspring of two of the most feared monsters in myth, Echidna and Typhon, and was the brother of the Hydra and the Sphinx. Cerberus was one of the hybrids loved by ancient artists, a huge dog with many heads, usually three but sometimes as many as 50. All the heads were wrapped up in a mane of living snakes. As guard dog of the underworld, Cerberus preserved the boundary between life and death, resisting the efforts of heroes who tried to enter the underworld while still alive. Despite his ferocity, Cerberus could be defeated, albeit only temporarily. Orpheus sang him to sleep when he tried to bring back Eurydice, and both Aeneas and Theseus drugged Cerberus with cake. Unfortunately for Theseus, the drug wore off before he could get back out, and he was trapped until Heracles rescued him. Heracles' approach was more direct. He simply overpowered Cerberus, wrestling him to the ground. As the capture of Cerberus was one of the labors set by Eurystheus, Heracles took him to Mycenae, but Eurystheus was so terrified that he hid in a large pot and ordered Heracles to return Cerberus to Hades.

3-SECOND MUSE
Cerberus, a monstrous dog with many heads, guarded the entrance to the underworld, keeping the dead from the living and also the living from the dead.

3-MINUTE ODYSSEY
Snakes symbolized the relationship between life and death. Medusa had snakes for hair, the Chimaera had a snake's tail, Echidna was half woman and half snake, and many figures died from snake bites, including Orpheus' wife, Eurydice.

RELATED MYTH
Where Cerberus keeps people from escaping from Hades, the snake in the Garden of Eden myth (Genesis 3) causes the eviction of the original humans from paradise.

3-SECOND BIOGRAPHIES
HADES
Name given both to the underworld and to its king
See page 82

HERACLES/HERCULES
Son of Alcmene and Zeus, became a god after death
See page 96

THESEUS
Founding King of Athens
See page 106

ORPHEUS
Tried to guide his wife Eurydice back from Hades
See page 120

30-SECOND TEXT
Emma Griffiths

The many-headed guardian of the underworld, Cerberus is a frequent foe of Greek heroes.

POLYPHEMUS
& THE CYCLOPES

the 30-second mythology

Returning from Troy, Odysseus

and his companions came to an unknown land. They made their way to a cave, and presently a Cyclops returned with his flocks, closing the mouth of the cave with a great boulder. When the Cyclops, Polyphemus, asked the strangers who they were, Odysseus explained that they were Greeks on their way home from Troy. Polyphemus responded by seizing a couple of the men and devouring them. The Greeks felt helpless, for even if they could kill the giant, they could not push aside the rock that blocked the mouth of the cave. The next morning Polyphemus ate another couple of men. In the evening the giant asked Odysseus his name and Odysseus said he was called "Nobody." After the Cyclops fell asleep, the men poked out his eye with a great pointed stake, and Polyphemus awoke, crying out to the other Cyclopes for help, saying that Nobody had injured him. The other Cyclopes assumed he had gone crazy. In the morning Polyphemus let his animals out to pasture, feeling among them to make sure the Greeks did not try to escape with them. To avoid detection, however, the Greeks had attached themselves to the undersides of the sheep and slipped out along with the flock.

3-SECOND MUSE
Polyphemus, one of the single-eyed giants known collectively as Cyclopes, was a son of the Greek god Poseidon and the sea nymph Thoosa.

3-MINUTE ODYSSEY
There were two different groups of Cyclopes in Greek mythology, apparently unrelated to each other. One set were blacksmiths who forged thunderbolts for Zeus. They consisted of three brothers, sons of Gaia (earth) and Uranus (sky). The other set were the cannibalistic shepherds whom Odysseus encountered on his way home from Troy. Both groups of Cyclopes were giants with a single eye in the middle of their forehead.

RELATED MYTH
Polyphemus plays the role of the "stupid ogre," or slow-witted adversary, who is outwitted by the protagonist. An example of a stupid ogre in Nordic myth is the giant Thrym, who is tricked by the god Thor.

3-SECOND BIOGRAPHIES
THE MINOTAUR
Monstrous being who was part human and part bull
See page 62

MEDUSA & THE GORGONS
Monstrous female beings with snakes for hair
See page 64

CERBERUS
Multi-headed dog of Hades
See page 66

30-SECOND TEXT
William Hansen

Polyphemus' brute strength proves no match for the cunning of Odysseus.

March 20, 43 BCE
Born Sulmona, Italy

29–25 BCE
Took up poetry full time

25 BCE
His first recitation

19 BCE
Composed *Heroides*
(*The Heroines*)

16–15 BCE
Composed *Amores*
(*The Loves*)

8–3 BCE
Second edition of *Amores*

2 CE
Composed *Ars Amatoria*
(*The Art of Love*) and
Remedia Amoris (*The
Cure for Love*)

8 CE
Composed
Metamorphoses; began
work on *Fasti*

8 CE
Exiled to Tomis (modern
Constantza, Romania)

9–12 CE
Composed *Tristia*

17/18 CE
Died in exile

2004
Metamorphoses
translated by David
Raeburn

OVID

Ovid (Publius Ovidius Naso) is one of the best-loved Roman poets. He was immensely popular in his own time, and much imitated by medieval writers.

One of his most popular works, still read today and a source for much of what we know about classical mythology, is the mock-epic *Metamorphoses*, which gives Ovid's original take on 250 myths. The theme of this work is that everything in the cosmos is transitory. There is no one main figure in the work, and even the roughly chronological order is often ignored. The key metamorphosis is of gods acting like, and so almost becoming, humans at the beginning of the work and of humans becoming gods at the end. In between are almost invariably unhappy relations, spurred by love or the failure of it, between gods and humans on the one hand and between humans and humans on the other.

We know a good deal about Ovid because he tells us a lot about himself. Trained as a lawyer, he turned to poetry when he was about 19. A friend of Horace and on distant nodding terms with Virgil, Ovid became the master of the elegiac couplet (a form of lyric poetry). His first major work, *Heroides* (*The Heroines*), was a collection of fictional love letters from mythical heroines to their feckless, absent, or absconding lovers. There followed *Amores* (*The Loves*), a series of amorous epistles to a fictional lover, Corinna, but his true blockbuster was undoubtedly *Ars Amatoria* (*The Art of Love*), a three-volume guide to love, seduction, and sex for both genders. Ovid then wrote the sequel *Remedia Amoris* (*The Cure for Love*). Also extant is a fragment of *Medicamina Faciei Feminae* (*Treatments for Women's Faces*), probably the first book of beauty tips for women.

Metamorphoses was completed in 8 CE, just before Ovid was exiled to the Black Sea by Augustus. Perhaps he was exiled because of his enthusiasm for adultery at a time when Rome was encouraging monogamy, or perhaps his exile was for political reasons. Sadly, he died in exile, leaving unfinished his magnum opus, *Fasti* (*The Festivals*)—an expression of Augustan ideals based on the Roman calendar.

THE HARPIES

the 30-second mythology

The Harpies' first appearance in Greek literature is incongruously charming. For Hesiod, they are goddesses of the scudding storm clouds, "lovely-haired," keeping pace "on their swift wings with the blasts of the winds and the birds." Later the nastier implications of their name "Snatchers" take over. The classical Harpies are monsters, birds with women's faces, with filthy tempers and filthier habits, shrieking voices and rapacious claws that snatch and carry off anything or anyone. As "hounds of Zeus," they were sent to torment the blind prophet, King Phineus, who had revealed too many of Zeus' secrets, by snatching away the food from his hands and covering his remaining food with foul droppings. Jason's Argonauts came to the starving king's rescue, and the two winged sons of the North Wind chased the Harpies away to the Strophades islands. There they later confronted Aeneas and his followers with taunting prophecies of starvation. As an emblem of grasping greed and shrill malice, the description "harpy" has been applied to politicians, lawyers, and tax collectors but it is now almost always a sexist put-down for an insufficiently self-effacing woman.

3-SECOND MUSE
The Harpies—their name means "Snatchers"—are demonic bird-women. They are emblems of cruelty and rapacity, and are personifications of storm winds.

3-MINUTE ODYSSEY
Virgil places the Harpies at the gate of the underworld, and in Dante's *Inferno* they haunt the Wood of the Suicides, maliciously tearing at the bark and leaves of the suicidal souls who have been transformed into trees. They make a memorable modern appearance in Philip Pullman's *His Dark Materials: The Amber Spyglass* as warders of the land of the dead, cruel and taunting but hungry for true stories of the world above.

RELATED MYTH
The Harpies, while uniquely Greek, are like Celtic goddesses of war and death, who often appeared in the form of predatory ravens or crows.

3-SECOND BIOGRAPHIES
ZEUS/JUPITER
King of Olympus, god of the sky
See page 32

AENEAS
Trojan hero and ancestor of the Romans
See page 104

JASON & MEDEA
Questing hero, leader of the Argonauts, and his wife
See page 122

30-SECOND TEXT
Geoffrey Miles

Monstrous birds with women's heads, the Harpies are the vicious, malicious "hounds of Zeus."

THE ERINYES

the 30-second mythology

The Erinyes were deities of
vengeance, who in some versions of myth
were born out of the blood that fell to the earth
(Gaia) when Cronus castrated his father, Uranus.
Other stories make them the children of Nyx,
goddess of the night. The Greeks considered
them numerous. The Romans, who called them
the Furies, assumed just three, who were named
Alecto, Tisiphone, and Megaera. They punished
mortals who committed the unnatural act of
killing a blood relative, and represented the
horror of kin-killing. Born as old women with
claws instead of hands and with snakes instead
of hair, they hunted offenders like animals and
drove them mad with binding incantations.
Their most famous victims were Alcmaeon and
Orestes, who had committed matricide to
avenge their fathers. In his play *The Eumenides*
Aeschylus presents them as pursuing Orestes
until Athena pacifies them and replaces their
regime of vengeance with a legal system of
justice. The Erinyes could also be called upon
by a parent's curse to punish a child. Amyntor
cursed his son Phoenix for sleeping with his
mistress, Althaia cursed her son Meleager after
he killed her brothers, and Oedipus is said to
have cursed his sons when they imprisoned him
after his incest and parricide were revealed.

RELATED MYTH
The Erinyes were like the
Gorgons, three sisters with
snakes for hair who turned
to stone any person who
saw them.

3-SECOND BIOGRAPHIES
URANUS
Sky father to Gaia's
earth mother
See page 22

DELPHI
Home to the Delphic Oracle
See page 90

AESCHYLUS
Fifth-century Athenian
tragic playwright
See page 100

OEDIPUS
King of Thebes who killed his
father and married his mother
See page 116

30-SECOND TEXT
Emma Griffiths

*Known to the
Romans as the Furies,
these sisters exact
vengeance for, above
all, either parricide
or matricide.*

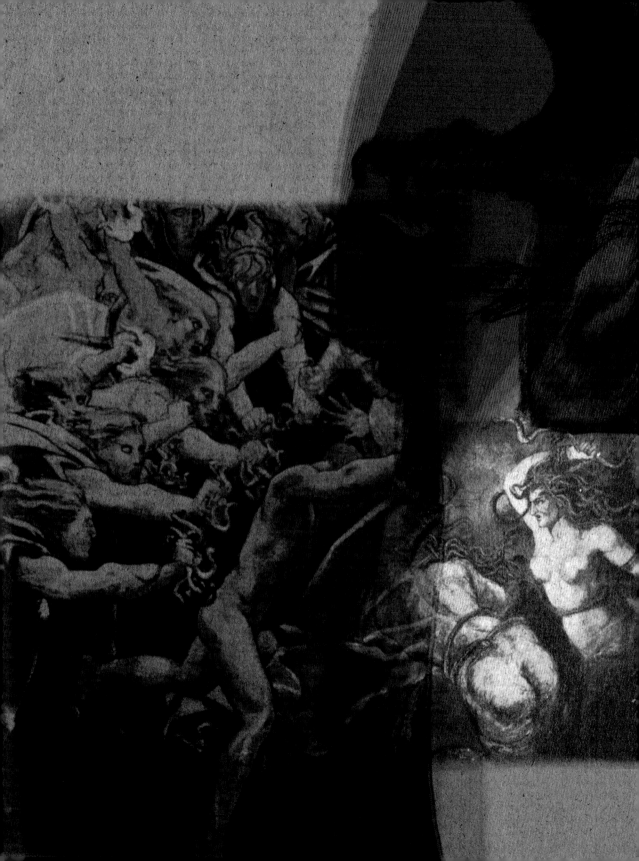

GEOGRAPHY

Achaeans People who lived in the north Peloponnesian region of Achaea during the Mycenaean period. The term is used by Homer to refer to the various groups that made up the collective Greek force that besieged Troy. The Achaean League was a confederacy of 12 city-states from the region.

ambrosia Term used to describe the food of the Olympian gods. In most but not all cases, ambrosia is what the gods ate, while nectar is what they drank. The gods would often feed ambrosia to their horses, and Athena gave Heracles ambrosia when he became immortal. The King of Phrygia, Tantalus, having been invited to eat with the gods, was banished to Tartarus for, among other things, attempting to steal ambrosia to give to his human subjects.

cosmos From the Greek word *kosmos* (literally "order" or "beauty"). In ancient Greek cosmogony, the cosmos emerged out of the vast emptiness of Chaos, the primordial state of matter. In contrast to the Bible, in which God creates the world by himself but not out of himself, the Greek view of creation, found above all in Hesiod's *Theogony*, is that the emergence of gods is identical with the creation of the world.

Muses Goddesses who inspired creativity in music, dance, literature, art, and science and from which are derived the words music, museum, and mosaic. To inspire meant to infuse with creativity but not to impart the content, as in revelation. There are usually considered to be nine muses, each of whom is sometimes given responsibility for a specific art. For Hesiod, the muses were the daughters of Zeus and Mnemosyne the goddess associated with memory. In other versions they are depicted as the early, primordial offspring of Gaia and Uranus.

nectar The liquid sustenance of the gods of Olympus.

prophecies Predictions delivered through oracles, such as those at Dodona and Delphi. Much store was set by oracular announcements despite their often being ambiguous. One of the most notorious examples of ambiguous prophecy involved a young Oedipus, who was informed that if he returned home, he would kill his father and sleep with his mother. The home that Oedipus assumed was being referred to was his present home, Corinth. To avoid the dread prophecy he set off for Thebes, the place of his birth—and the rest is history. Prophecies also came in dreams. While accepted as true, prophecies, it was believed, could also be averted—as the case of Oedipus and his father, Laius, illustrated. They were wrong.

psychopomp Name given to an entity that guides newly deceased souls to the afterlife. Psychopomps are found in many religions. Classical examples are Charon, Hermes, Hecate, and Morpheus.

Trojan Horse The giant wooden horse in which 30 Greek soldiers, including Odysseus, gained access to Troy. Under Odysseus' orders, the Greeks constructed the giant horse ostensibly to honor the goddess Athena, whose temple they had destroyed during the war, and thereby to ensure safe passage back to Greece. The Greek fleet then appeared to set sail home. The Trojans, tricked by Sinon, dragged the horse into the city and proceeded to celebrate the Greeks' departure. Sinon later opened the horse to let out the soldiers, who then opened the city gates to admit the returning Greek forces and bring about the sacking of Troy.

MOUNT OLYMPUS

the 30-second mythology

3-SECOND MUSE
Mount Olympus was
the mountain of the
gods, where they lived
in a beautiful palace in
endless feasting under
the watchful Zeus.

3-MINUTE ODYSSEY
Otus ("doom") and
Ephialtes ("nightmare")
were sons of Poseidon.
The brothers decided to
attack Mount Olympus.
To get high enough, they
piled Mount Ossa and
Mount Pelion, other
mountains of Thessaly,
on top of one another.
Artemis jumped between
them in the form of a deer.
Casting their spears, they
missed and instead struck
each other dead.

At 9,570 feet (2,917 meters),
Mount Olympus is the tallest mountain in
Greece and one of the highest peaks in Europe.
It is part of the range that separates the plain
of Macedonia from Thessaly. No ancient Greek
ever climbed it, as far as we know, and in the
poetic imagination it was the home of the gods.
There, high above the clouds, the Olympians
had their palace, except for Poseidon and
Hades, who dwelled in the sea and in the
underworld. The gods spent their time dining
on ambrosia, a magical food, and drinking
nectar, a magical drink (both words probably
mean "deathless"). As they feasted, Apollo sang
and played his lyre, much as the oral poets
entertained at earthly courts, with the Muses
accompanying him in choral song. When the
sun went down, the gods retired to their private
dwellings, built by Hephaestus. Although the
gods on Olympus lived eternally in a divine
paradise, Olympus was very much part of earth
rather than a transcendent, spiritual place.

RELATED MYTH
The biblical Tower of
Babel was an attempt to
reach and thereby equal,
if not overthrow, God.

3-SECOND BIOGRAPHIES
ZEUS/JUPITER
King of Olympus, god
of the sky
See page 32

HERA/JUNO
Queen of the gods, wife
of Zeus/Jupiter
See page 34

HEPHAESTUS/VULCAN
God of crafts, blacksmith
to the gods
See page 38

APOLLO
God of music, prophecy,
and, later, the sun
See page 42

30-SECOND TEXT
Barry B. Powell

*The home of most of
the gods, Olympus is a
paradise of continual
feasting and music.*

HADES

the 30-second mythology

According to Greek mythology,

nearly all human beings proceeded after death to a subterranean realm ruled by the dreaded king and queen of the dead, Hades and his wife Persephone. The realm was known as the House of Hades, suggesting a built structure, or simply Hades. Another common name was Erebus (ancient Greek, "darkness"), which implied a murky region where the souls of the dead roamed. Within Hades there were streams and lakes with names identifying misery, such as Acheron ("grief"), Cocytus ("wailing"), and Phlegethon ("burning"). Although the waters of the Styx ("hateful") are widely regarded as separating Hades from the land of the living, it was across the Acheron that the ferryman Charon transported newly deceased souls for a fee. Alternatively, Hermes Psychopompos ("Escorter-of-Souls") led the souls of the dead through the air to their new abode. Once the dead entered through Hades' gate, they were prevented from leaving by Hades' many headed hell hound, Cerberus. Although the souls resembled their former selves, so that they were recognizable and retained their personalities and memories, they had no more substance than smoke or reflections in water. They could enjoy no sensory pleasures and did not eat, converse, or reflect. Instead, they spent eternity inactive in a realm of darkness.

3-SECOND MUSE
In Greek cosmogony (relating to the origin of the universe), Hades was the place where humans resided after death, and also the name of the ruler of the dead.

3-MINUTE ODYSSEY
The House of Hades was not primarily a realm of punishment or reward, but merely the place where humans went when they died, whether they had led moral or immoral lives. Nevertheless, a few souls remained embodied and experienced exceptional treatment, for better or worse. For example, Sisyphus had the never-ending task of rolling a stone up a hill over and over again, while the renowned hunter Orion happily passed his time hunting game.

RELATED MYTH
A realm in which mortals carry on an existence of some kind after death is found in many mythologies. Examples are the House of Yama (India), Sheol (Israel), Niflheim (Scandinavia), and House of Donn (Ireland).

3-SECOND BIOGRAPHIES
CERBERUS
Multi-headed dog of Hades
See page 66

TARTARUS
Cosmic prison for defeated gods and monsters
See page 86

HERACLES/HERCULES
Greek hero of immense strength
See page 96

30-SECOND TEXT
William Hansen

The underground realm is presided over by its namesake, the king of the dead.

480 BCE
Born at Salamis, Greece

455 BCE
First City Dionysia competition

441 BCE
Won first prize at City Dionysia

C. 406 BCE
Died in Macedonia

405 BCE
The Bacchae and *Iphigenia in Aulis* performed at the City Dionysia, and took first prize

C. 200 CE
Ten of Euripides' plays published in text form

1955
Alcestis translated by Richmond Lattimore; *The Medea* translated by Rex Warner; *The Heracleidae* translated by Ralph Gladstone; *Hippolytus* translated by David Grene

EURIPIDES

Following Aeschylus and

Sophocles, Euripides was the last of the three great Greek tragedians, and probably the one most familiar to modern audiences. This is partly because 18 or so of the possible 92 plays he wrote survive intact, with many performances taking place today. His plots are more complex than those of Aeschylus or Sophocles. He marginalizes the chorus far more than either of them did. He develops his characters even more fully than they did. Above all, he "psychologizes" his characters, ascribing to them realistic, if still lamentable, motives. Of him, it has been commonly said that he writes about humans as they are and not as they ought to be.

In half of his plays Euripides introduces the sudden appearance at the end of a play of a god suspended from a crane—the technique know as *deus ex machina* ("god out of the machine"). The god serves to resolve an otherwise remaining confusion in the play. Ancient literary critics like Aristotle criticized the practice on the grounds that resolution should come from the story itself and not from something external imported into the story.

Scholars debate whether Euripides actually believed in the gods. If not, *deus ex machina* is almost a caricature of standard deference to gods. At the least, Euripides castigates the gods as cruel, capricious, and above all irrational. Seen this way, he wants to reform,

not reject, divinity. In his refusal to genuflect before the gods, he breaks with both Aeschylus and Sophocles. At the most, Euripides dismisses as irrational the belief in gods themselves. When he is taken to be going this far, he is translating the gods into projections of human characteristics, which is what Friedrich Nietzsche and Sigmund Freud both did in modern times. Nietzsche himself assumes that Euripides is not an atheist and that his enlistment of a *deus ex machina* is intended to vindicate them as forces of rationality and moderation.

Euripides was the least popular of the three major tragedians. He won only five prizes at the City Dionysia drama festivals, and one of those posthumously. One reason for this might have been his brave and provocative sympathy for women, especially for those mistreated by men. He presents a gallery of powerful, though flawed, heroines. One of his most celebrated heroines is Medea, who saves her husband Jason's life only to be abandoned by him for someone else. Another celebrated heroine is Electra, who abets her brother, Orestes, in the killing of their mother, Clytemnestra. Euripides' unrelenting condemnation of war doubtless also made him unpopular.

We know little about Euripides' personal life other than that he was married twice and allegedly wrote his plays in what is now the Cave of Euripides in Syracuse.

TARTARUS

the 30-second mythology

Tartarus is the lowest of the worlds that make up the cosmos. Hesiod claims that if a bronze anvil should fall from the sky, it would land on the earth ten days later, and if it should fall from the earth, it would likewise reach Tartarus on the tenth day. Tartarus is therefore as far beneath the earth as the earth is beneath the sky. Tartarus serves as a cosmic prison. Gods and monsters can be defeated, but since they are supernatural beings, they are ordinarily not subject to death. What are the ruling gods to do with powerful enemies they have vanquished but cannot kill? They put them in indefinite storage in Tartarus. It is there that the Olympian gods imprisoned their adversaries, the Titans, and it is there that Zeus confined the huge monster Typhon after their combat. Since the prisoners are strong, Tartarus is surrounded by a bronze wall, and since the prisoners are huge, Tartarus is necessarily vast. According to Hesiod, a person entering through its bronze door would be tossed about in the darkness by great winds for a full year before reaching its bottom. Tartarus is also the prison for those human beings who have most insulted or challenged the gods, such as Tantalus and Sisyphus.

3-SECOND MUSE
Tartarus is a vast, underworld prison for defeated gods and monsters, and also for some humans.

3-MINUTE ODYSSEY
Like other parts of the mythic cosmos such as Gaia (Earth), Uranus (Sky), and Hades (land of the dead), Tartarus is at once a place and a personality. As a place, Tartarus is a prison. As a personality, Tartarus is the son of Gaia, with whom he mates.

RELATED MYTH
In many mythic traditions supernatural beings can only be confined and not slain. For example, in Nordic myth the god Loki and the huge wolf Fenrir are fettered by the ruling gods.

3-SECOND BIOGRAPHIES
GAIA
Mother earth
See page 18

URANUS
Father sky
See page 22

HADES
Realm of the dead
See page 82

30-SECOND TEXT
William Hansen

Tartarus is both a personality in his own right and the domain that he controls.

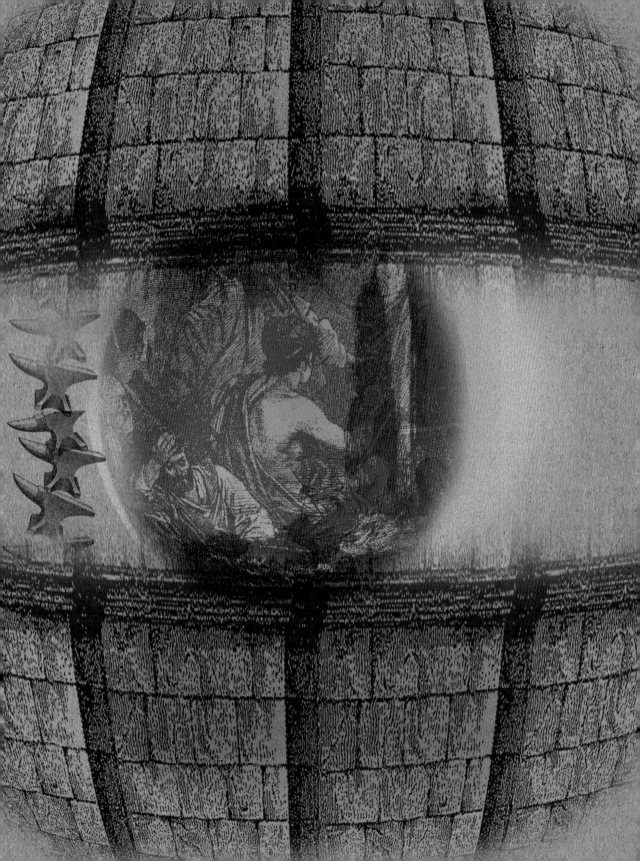

TROY

the 30-second mythology

According to Greek mythology,

Troy was a major trading city on the western coast of modern-day Turkey and the scene of an epic war "between the Trojans, tamers of horses, and the bronze-clad Achaeans." The war began when Paris, son of the Trojan King Priam, went in quest of the most beautiful woman in the world, and came back with Helen, wife of the Spartan King Menelaus. In response, Agamemnon, Menelaus' brother, led a thousand Greek ships on a "shock and awe" expedition against Troy. But like the current war in Iraq, the siege lasted for many years. Heroes on both sides—Hector, Achilles, Ajax—fought, quarreled, and died beneath Troy's massive walls, and all the while the gods watched and interfered. Eventually, the city, which had resisted force, fell to cunning. The wily Odysseus constructed the original "Trojan Horse"—a giant wooden trophy that the Trojans triumphantly dragged into their city, unaware that it contained Greek soldiers. Troy fell in flames, Menelaus reclaimed Helen, and the Greeks—some of them—returned home. From Homer through Euripides, Virgil, Chaucer, and Shakespeare to the 2004 movie *Troy*, the Trojan War has become our most iconic image of the glory, brutality, and tragedy of war.

3-SECOND MUSE
Troy was a legendary city besieged for ten years by the Greeks. The Trojan War has become the archetypal war story in Western culture.

3-MINUTE ODYSSEY
While the ancient Greeks assumed that Troy and the Trojan War were real, historians believed that both were made up. Then, in the 1870s, the German archaeologist-adventurer Heinrich Schliemann claimed to have uncovered the ruins of Troy at Hissarlik in Turkey. Excavations on a grand scale continue, and most experts assume that Troy did exist and that a battle involving a siege likely took place; but whether an event on the scale described in the *Iliad* occurred remains questionable.

RELATED MYTH
Legends of similarly epic proportions in other cultures include the Indian *Mahabharata*, the German *Nibelungenlied*, and the French *Chanson de Roland*.

3-SECOND BIOGRAPHIES
HOMER
Early Greek epic poet, author of the *Iliad* and *Odyssey*
See page 44

ACHILLES
Greek warrior, hero of the *Iliad*
See page 98

ODYSSEUS/ULYSSES
King of Ithaca and great strategist of the Trojan War
See page 102

AENEAS
Trojan hero, ancestor of the Romans
See page 104

30-SECOND TEXT
Geoffrey Miles

The conquest of Troy is one of the most enduring tales in all of mythology.

DELPHI

the 30-second mythology

Delphi was the belly button of the mythological universe. Zeus conducted an aerial survey using two eagles to find the center of the world, and the place where the eagles met was marked with a stone called an *omphalos* (Greek for "navel"). The most famous location for this meeting point was Delphi, a religious center initially dedicated to the goddesses Gaia, Themis, and Phoebe before the site passed to Apollo after he killed the snake Python. Apollo's prophecies were conveyed through the Pythian priestess, who entered a trance, possibly aided by chewing bay leaves. Archaeologists have suggested that the geology of Delphi may have inspired the myth, as hallucinogenic gases rose from the deep chasm in the cliff. On the one hand the oracle in myth could be very specific. For example, Oedipus' father Laius was told that if he had a child, this son would kill his father. On the other hand the oracle was renowned for giving ambiguous meanings. Oedipus, having been told that he was not the son of the King and Queen of Corinth, asked the oracle who his real parents were. He was informed only that he would kill his father and marry his mother. Assuming the oracle was referring to his present, Corinthian parents, he immediately fled Corinth for Thebes.

3-SECOND MUSE
Delphi was home of the Delphic Oracle, a sacred site where Apollo delivered prophecies through the voice of the Pythian priestess.

3-MINUTE ODYSSEY
The temple of Apollo at Delphi had two mottoes: "Nothing in excess" and "Know thyself." The ambiguous, oracular advice may reflect the importance of these psychological warnings. A similar warning may be taken from the myth of Cassandra: Apollo gave her the gift of prophecy when she promised to sleep with him. But when she did not, he added a curse that her prophecies would never be believed.

RELATED MYTH
The role of the Castellian spring, used for purification at Delphi, recalls the Norse myth of the prophet Mimir, who protected the sacred well beneath the Tree of the World.

3-SECOND BIOGRAPHIES
ZEUS/JUPITER
King of Olympus, god of the sky
See page 32

APOLLO
God of the sun, music, and poetry
See page 42

OEDIPUS
Tragic Greek figure, who killed his father and married his mother
See page 116

30-SECOND TEXT
Emma Griffiths

The center of the world, Delphi is the spiritual heartland of Apollo and home of the Delphic Oracle.

HEROES ◑

HEROES
GLOSSARY

Aeneid Virgil's epic poem, which recounts the story of Aeneas, a Trojan prince, who, after a series of adventures, eventually establishes a settlement in Latium, thereby founding what becomes Rome. Organized into 12 books and written between 29 and 19 BCE, the poem borrows from the *Odyssey* and *Iliad*. At the same time it makes reference and pays tribute to the deeds and rule of Virgil's own Emperor Augustus.

centaurs Half-man, half-horse creatures, who exemplify untamed, wild nature. They are often depicted as the lustful, drunken followers of Dionysus. An exception is the centaur Chiron, who is a tutor to various heroes, including Achilles, Ajax, Theseus, and, in some versions, Heracles, who was known for his intelligence and not just for his strength. While the centaurs were usually depicted as males, there were occasionally female centaurs.

Elysium (the Elysian Fields) A region of the underworld which, unlike Hades, is the equivalent of heaven. Whereas practically everyone went to Hades—except for those consigned to Tartarus—only a few went to Elysium, which was the final resting place for heroes or those deemed especially dutiful. An example is Aeneas' father, Anchises, who is described by Virgil as living in a realm of perpetual spring. According to one source, Cronus ruled over Elysium. Although Elysium is mentioned in the *Odyssey*, Odysseus never visited. By contrast, Aeneas in Virgil's *Aeneid* went there to confer with his father, Anchises.

Graeae Two or usually three sisters of the Gorgons. They shared a single eye and tooth. They were the daughters of Phorcys and Ceto and, like their parents, were ancient sea goddesses. Usually portrayed as old, gray hags, though sometimes with the bodies of swans, they had their eye and tooth stolen by Perseus, who then forced them to tell him of their Gorgon sisters' whereabouts.

Iliad Homer's epic poem, which recounts a few months during the last year of the Trojan War, although there are many past references to prior events. Written in around 800 BCE, the poem is arranged into 24 books, and deals with the nearly universal themes of fate and free will, divinity and humanity, pride and glory, compassion and love and hate, and life and death. It is one of the most influential works of Western literature.

River Styx Perhaps the best known to modern audiences of the rivers that flow through the underworld realm of Hades. The Styx was said to flow around Hades seven or nine times and to form the boundary between the living and the dead. Considered sacred even by the gods themselves, it was the river in which Thetis dipped her son Achilles when an infant, thereby making his body invincible—apart from the heel by which she held him.

Sirens Three sea nymphs who used an irresistible song to lure sailors to their deaths on the rocks close to the island where they lived. Demeter cursed them with the bodies of birds for failing to prevent her daughter Persephone's abduction by Hades. Jason and his Argonauts avoided disaster when the Sirens sang thanks to Orpheus, whose playing drowned them out. Odysseus ordered his men to block their ears so that they could not hear them, but he had himself tied to the mast so that he could hear but would be able to resist.

Twelve labors The 12 challenges that Heracles had to undertake as punishment for killing his wife and children during a fit of madness caused by his erstwhile enemy Hera. Having recovered his senses and witnessed his crime, Heracles traveled to Delphi to ask the oracle how he could atone. He was told, he must serve under King Eurystheus for 12 years, who set Heracles the labors. Traditionally the labors were: 1) killing the Nemean lion; 2) killing the Lernaean Hydra; 3) capturing the hind of Ceryneia; 4) capturing the Erymanthian boar; 5) cleaning the Augean stables; 6) driving away the Stymphalian birds; 7) capturing the Cretan bull; 8) stealing the man-eating horses of Diomedes; 9) stealing the belt of the Hippolyte; 10) capturing the cattle of Geryon; 11) stealing the apples of the Hesperides; and 12) capturing Cerberus.

HERACLES/ HERCULES

the 30-second mythology

3-SECOND MUSE
Heracles, known in Rome
as Hercules, was the son
of Zeus and Alcmena. The
most celebrated of the
classical heroes, he
transcended mortality and
joined the Olympian gods.

3-MINUTE ODYSSEY
Heracles was noted not
only for his extraordinary
feats of strength and
endurance, but also for
his intelligence, skills, and
musicianship. Among his
traits were an excessive
temper, a sexual prowess
that once saw him
deflower 50 maidens in
a single night, and a
tendency toward spells
of madness that produced
atrocities, the worst of
which was the killing of
his children and his wife
Megara. His accepted
punishment was his
twelve labors.

As the "Glory of Hera," which is what "Heracles" means, the hero was linked by name to Hera, the greatest of his persecutors. Humiliated by her husband Zeus' escapade with another woman, she worked against Heracles even before his birth. She secured for Eurystheus, his mortal victimizer, the kingship that Zeus had intended for Heracles. When Hera put serpents in Heracles' cot to kill him, he killed them instead, demonstrating the strength that would later get him through his various exploits, not least the twelve labors. These labors took him from his Peloponnesian homeland to exotic locations, not least the edge of the earth and the underworld. Heracles died, effectively, at the hands of one of his long dead victims: the centaur Nessus, whom he had killed while Nessus was trying to rape his wife, Deianira. Believing it to be a love potion, Deianira gave Heracles a robe soaked in Nessus' blood; as its poison was eating into his flesh, Heracles insisted upon being thrown upon his funeral pyre. After he died, Athena conveyed him by chariot to Mount Olympus. The marriage of Heracles to Hebe symbolized his divine rebirth while also marking his reconciliation with Hebe's mother, his erstwhile enemy Hera.

RELATED MYTH
Heracles was regarded
in antiquity as comparable
with Melqart, the "Thasian
Heracles" (Herodotus 2.44).
There are also parallels with
the biblical figures Samson
and Goliath.

3-SECOND BIOGRAPHIES
ZEUS/JUPITER
King of Olympus, god
of the sky
See page 32

HERA/JUNO
Queen of the gods, wife
of Zeus/Jupiter
See page 34

30-SECOND TEXT
Susan Deacy

The greatest of the heroes, Heracles is best known for his twelve labors. The first was wrestling a famous lion and the last was bringing the hell hound Cerberus to the surface of the earth.

αβγδεζηθια

Β

ACHILLES

the 30-second mythology

Achilles was the son of Peleus, the mortal King of the Myrmidons, and Thetis, a nymph, who tried to make the baby Achilles immortal by dipping him in the River Styx. Unfortunately, she overlooked the spot on his heel by which she held him in the river, thereby leaving him vulnerable to a mortal injury in that place. Achilles was given a choice by the gods: either to have a short life filled with glory or to have a long life lived in obscurity. He chose the first option and became the greatest Greek warrior in the Trojan War. Homer's epic poem the *Iliad* tells of Achilles' anger when he was insulted by King Agamemnon, who took away a slave woman given to him as a battle prize. Achilles refused to fight. But when the Greeks began to suffer losses, his friend Patroclus begged to borrow his armor and fight. Patroclus fought well but was killed by Achilles' Trojan counterpart, Hector. In a rage Achilles not only killed Hector but also defiled his body and relented only when Hector's father, Priam, came to beg for its return. Near the end of the Trojan War Achilles died when he was struck on the heel by an arrow fired by another Trojan prince, Paris.

3-SECOND MUSE
The greatest fighter of the Trojan War, he chose a short life of glory over a long life in obscurity.

3-MINUTE ODYSSEY
In some versions of the myth, Achilles was transported to Elysium and married Medea, but in Homer's *Odyssey* the shade of Achilles appears to Odysseus and regrets his decision to die young and spend eternity in Hades. Although he is consoled when he hears from the visiting Odysseus about his son, Neoptolemos, his continuing sadness undermines the traditional epic insistence on the value of glory.

RELATED MYTH
The idea of a hero made invulnerable but for a single missed spot is also seen in the Teutonic story of Siegfried and the Indian story of Krishna.

3-SECOND BIOGRAPHIES
TROY
Legendary city-state and the location of the Trojan War
See page 88

ODYSSEUS/ULYSSES
King of Ithaca and great strategist of the Trojan War
See page 102

30-SECOND TEXT
Emma Griffiths

Achilles' superhuman skill as a fighter was compromised by his self-centeredness. Today, the "Achilles' heel" is a metaphor for a character flaw or imperfection in even the most celebrated mortal.

c. 525/4 BCE
Born at Eleusis, Greece

499 BCE
First performance of
a work

490 BCE
Fought at Battle of
Marathon

484 BCE
First victory at City
Dionysia

480 BCE
Fought at Battle of
Salamis

472 BCE
First production of *The
Persians* staged

472 BCE
Staged four plays,
financed by Pericles

467 BCE
First production of the
Seven Against Thebes

464 BCE
First production of *The
Suppliants*

458 BCE
First production of *The
Oresteia* staged

c. 445/6 BCE
Died at Syracuse, Sicily

1953
The Oresteia translated
by Richmond Lattimore

1977
The Oresteia translated
by Robert Fagles

AESCHYLUS

Aeschylus was the father of classical tragedy. His most celebrated successors, Sophocles and Euripides, made significant changes in the genre, but they built on his achievements. To be sure, Aeschylus himself inherited tragedy of a kind, but he transformed the genre by introducing a second actor, thereby increasing the dialogue and also making the chorus less important. He made the conventional trilogy into a unified set of plays. Previously, playwrights composed three separate plays plus a bawdy satyr play. Of Aeschylus' trilogies, only *The Oresteia* remains.

Thematically, Aeschylus' plays, of which only six or seven out of 70 or so survive, focus on human responsibility for actions. Aeschylus deems the standard appeal to Fate or to the gods an evasion of responsibility. At the same time he advocates devotion to the gods, to whom humans must submit, and sees them as more good than evil. He traces the development of the gods from wrathful forces into figures of mercy as well as justice. He berates gods as well as humans for excessive pride and espouses moderation. He believes that from suffering, which his characters invariably endure, can come wisdom.

Aeschylus' first play, *The Persians*, is about the Battle of Salamis and was unique in Greek tragedy in dealing with contemporary events. In *Seven Against Thebes* he blames humans themselves for parricide and incest rather than attributing them to a divine curse, which was the common explanation. His *Oresteia* tells the story of the life of King Agamemnon of Argos and of the destruction of him and his family. It is also the only complete extant trilogy of any classical Greek playwright.

Aeschylus was born at Eleusis, northwest of Athens. This city was famous for its cult of Demeter. Although an initiate into the cult of Demeter, he was inspired even more by Dionysus. Greek drama began in the Dionysia, which were festivals held in honor of the god. Aeschylus' work was very successful in its time—he won at the City Dionysia competitions 13 times—and is still widely performed today.

Yet Aeschylus was also a soldier. He fought at both Marathon and Salamis, defending Greece from the invading Persians. His epitaph ignores his contribution to the dramatic arts and concentrates on his military prowess.

ODYSSEUS/ULYSSES
the 30-second mythology

Perhaps the most famous example

of Odysseus' cunning, for which he was most celebrated, was the scheme he devised to end the siege of Troy. The Trojan Horse, in which he hid Greek warriors, has become a symbol for deception. However, Odysseus' cunning was not limited to Troy and to his many adventures en route home. Earlier, while on Ithaca, he had attempted to avoid joining Agamemnon's army by pretending to be mad. Yet for all his cunning, Odysseus was capable of moments of arrogance, as when, in sailing away from the island of the Cyclopes, he revealed his actual name to Polyphemus, the Cyclops he had just deceived. This disclosure brought upon him the wrath of Poseidon, Polyphemus' father, who, as the god of the sea, was well placed to impede Odysseus' journey home. Among the various females who doted upon Odysseus were the Phaeacian girl Nausicaa, who encouraged her people to become so well disposed to him when he was shipwrecked on their island that they provided him with ships for his voyage back to Ithaca. With Athena, meanwhile, he concocted the plot to defeat the suitors who had been occupying his place and courting his wife.

3-SECOND MUSE
Odysseus, known as Ulysses in Latin, was the hero whose cleverness enabled him to overcome what for anyone else would have been insurmountable obstacles to his return from the Trojan War.

3-MINUTE ODYSSEY
Odysseus' travels en route home took him as far as the edge of the ocean, where he encountered the shades of the dead. The living characters he met on his journey home included the enchantress Circe; the sweet-singing Sirens; whom Odysseus alone heard and lived to tell about; and the goddess Calypso, who kept him marooned for seven years as her beloved.

RELATED MYTH
Among the heroes whose adventures parallel Odysseus' are Aeneas and Sinbad the Sailor.

3-SECOND BIOGRAPHIES
POSEIDON/NEPTUNE
God of the sea and horses, brother to Zeus
See page 36

ATHENA/MINERVA
Goddess of wisdom, warfare, and justice
See page 52

POLYPHEMUS
The Cyclops son of Poseidon
See page 68

30-SECOND TEXT
Susan Deacy

Odysseus was so thoroughly distinguished for his unchecked scheming that he shared the epithet polymetis ("cunning in many ways") with his divine helper, Athena.

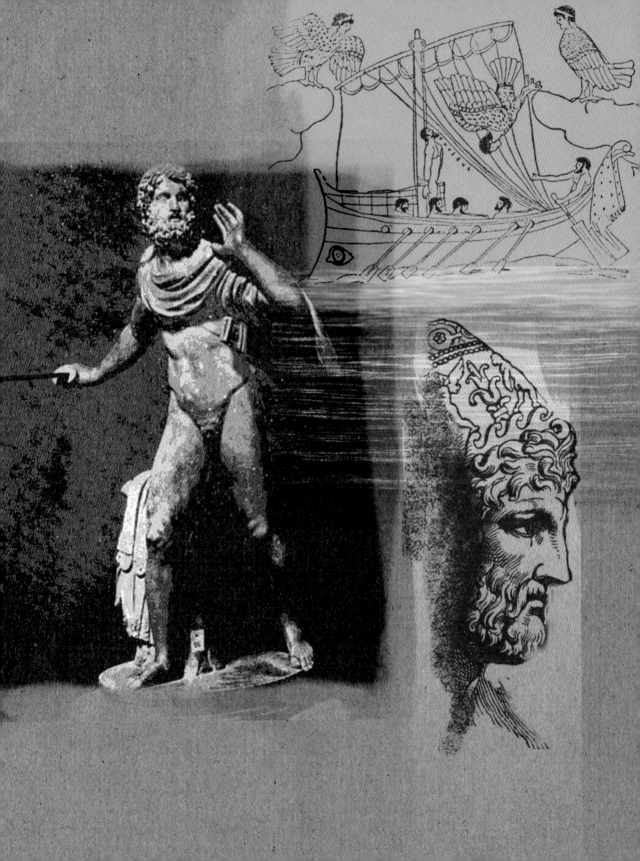

AENEAS

the 30-second mythology

3-SECOND MUSE
"Arms and the man I sing." The man was Aeneas, a Trojan prince, the human son of Venus (Aphrodite), destined to become the ancestor of the Romans.

3-MINUTE ODYSSEY
It took some creative handling of myth and history for Virgil, or his sources, to link the fall of Troy (12th century BCE) to the founding of Rome (traditionally 753 BCE); three centuries of kings had to be invented to bridge the gap from Aeneas to Romulus. An impossible love affair between Aeneas and Dido, founder of Carthage (eighth century BCE), supplied a mythic origin for the Punic Wars.

A secondary character in the *Iliad*, Aeneas is the main character in Virgil's Roman epic, the *Aeneid*. When Troy fell to the Greeks, Aeneas escaped, carrying his old father on his back and the images of the gods in his hands, with orders from Jupiter (Zeus) himself to lead the Trojan survivors to a new homeland and a historic destiny. Much like Odysseus, Aeneas wandered for years, storm tossed, chasing elusive prophecies. In Carthage, Aeneas and Queen Dido fell in love, but the gods said "move on!" and Dido killed herself. When he finally reached Italy, Aeneas was embroiled in another war against the local resistance leader, Turnus. At last he was able to found his new city, the precursor of Rome, though he did not live to enjoy it. Aeneas was a new kind of *Roman* hero, different from glorious Achilles or tricky Odysseus. Virgil's word for him is *pius*—self-denyingly driven by *pietas*, or duty to gods, family, and nation. He received from the gods a shield on which was engraved the future history of Rome, and "he takes up on his shoulder the destined fame of his descendants." He is a reluctant hero who must literally shoulder the burden of history. In death the gods made him immortal.

RELATED MYTH
Aeneas bears some likeness to the biblical Moses, another hero commanded by God to lead his followers in long wandering but who dies before entering the Promised Land.

3-SECOND BIOGRAPHIES
ZEUS/JUPITER
King of Olympus, god of the sky
See page 32

APHRODITE/VENUS
Goddess of love and beauty
See page 50

DIDO
Queen of Carthage, Aeneas' tragic lover
See page 126

VIRGIL
Roman epic poet, author of the *Aeneid*
See page 128

30-SECOND TEXT
Geoffrey Miles

Driven by duty, Aeneas was a new, Roman breed of hero.

THESEUS

the 30-second mythology

3-SECOND MUSE
Theseus was a culture hero, who helped civilize the world by ridding it of beasts. He was also hailed as a reformer for establishing the political system of Athens.

3-MINUTE ODYSSEY
Theseus was the product of a liaison on Sphairia between his mother, the Troezenian princess Aethra, and either the Athenian King Aegeas or the god Poseidon. He was born as a result of trickery, although the deceiver's identity varies, as does that of the victim. Either Pittheus, Aethra's father, made Aegeas drunk before getting him to sleep with Aethra, or Athena told Aethra to go to Sphairia, where, caught off guard, Poseidon slept with her.

When he reached manhood and lifted the boulder covering the sword and sandals of his father, Aegeus, Theseus demonstrated the strength that marked him as a hero in the mold of Heracles. Traveling to Athens to claim his birthright, he chose the overland route rather than the short sea crossing in order to slay the various brigands, rulers, and monsters that victimized the localities along the way. Having reached Athens, and having overcome his stepmother Medea's attempts to kill him, he managed to rid the city of its obligation to Minos. He sailed to Crete with a group of youths sent as offerings to the Minotaur but then killed the creature, aided by Ariadne, daughter of Minos. She escaped with him only to be abandoned on Naxos. When Theseus forgot to replace the black sail that would denote failure with a white one, Aegeus, thinking his son was dead, threw himself into the sea, which bore his name thereafter. Theseus' other adventures included an expedition to Amazonland and a failed attempt to abduct Persephone that left his accomplice, Perithous, stuck forever in Hades. Theseus' life ended when, like his father, he fell off a cliff, in his case pushed by Lycomedes.

RELATED MYTH
The theme of traveling to a distant land, defeating a monster, and escaping with the local maiden who assists is consistent with a widespread folktale motif of the "helper-maiden."

3-SECOND BIOGRAPHIES
POSEIDON/NEPTUNE
God of the sea and horses, brother to Zeus
See page 36

THE MINOTAUR
Monstrous being—part man, part bull
See page 62

HERACLES/HERCULES
Greek hero of immense strength
See page 96

30-SECOND TEXT
Susan Deacy

Like many other classical heroes, Theseus had a life that was both glorious and tragic.

PERSEUS

the 30-second mythology

Perseus' birth exemplified his father's ability to beget children in unusual guises, this time as the golden shower that infiltrated the tower in which Danaë was imprisoned. The reason for the imprisonment was a warning from an oracle received by Danaë's father, Acrisius, that her son would kill him. On discovering that Danaë had, despite his actions, borne a child, Acrisius cast the pair adrift in a chest. Some years later, Perseus traveled from Seriphos, the island where the chest had washed ashore and where he had then been raised by a fisherman whose brother was Polydectes, king of the island. Polydectes wanted Perseus out of the way so that he could marry Danaë, Perseus' mother. But Perseus succeeded in the deed that Polydectes had assumed would get him killed: beheading Medusa, the sole Gorgon who was mortal. He was helped by Athena and Hermes as well as by a triad of unwilling helpers, the Graeae, who were the sisters of the Gorgons. Further assistance came from the nymphs, who, according to some accounts, furnished him with four aids: the cap of invisibility normally worn by Hades, a pair of winged sandals that enabled him to fly to "Gorgonland" and later escape from Medusa's surviving sisters, an adamantine sickle to cut off Medusa's head, and a bag in which to store the head.

3-SECOND MUSE
Perseus was the Gorgon-slaying and damsel-rescuing son of Danaë, and of either Zeus or Proteus, Acrisius' brother.

3-MINUTE ODYSSEY
Perseus' adventures on his return journey from the home of the Gorgons included slaying the sea monster that was about to devour the girl Andromeda, who had been chained to a rock to avert the wrath of Poseidon after her mother had claimed to surpass the Nereids in beauty. Upon his return to Seriphos, Perseus showed the Gorgon's head to Polydectes, thereby turning him to stone. As the oracle had predicted, Perseus did eventually kill his grandfather—albeit by accident, with a discus.

RELATED MYTH
A hero encountering three elderly persons, who are often women and who sometimes share a single eye, is a folkloristic motif found in other cultures.

3-SECOND BIOGRAPHIES
ZEUS/JUPITER
King of Olympus, god of the sky
See page 32

ATHENA/MINERVA
Goddess of wisdom, warfare, and justice
See page 52

HERMES/MERCURY
Messenger of the gods
See page 54

MEDUSA AND THE GORGONS
Serpent-haired monsters
See page 64

30-SECOND TEXT
Susan Deacy

The product of one of Zeus' many illicit affairs, Perseus famously beheads the Gorgon Medusa.

TRAGIC FIGURES

Argonauts Named after the ship in which they sailed, the *Argo*, the Argonauts were a group of heroic adventurers who joined Jason on his voyage to Colchis (modern Georgia) in search of the Golden Fleece. Their number varies from source to source, but most accounts suggest there were around 50. Often included among them were Heracles, Orpheus, and Theseus. Ancient Greeks often claimed descent from the named Argonauts.

Golden Fleece The fleece of a golden, winged ram that was required by Jason in order for him to accede to the throne of Iolcus. Many years earlier, the ram had been sent by Hermes to save the lives of a king's son and daughter, whose jealous stepmother had plotted to kill them. The ram carried them off on its back, but the daughter, Helle, fell into the sea (hence Hellespont) before reaching the safety of Colchis (modern Georgia). The son sacrificed the ram to Zeus, and its fleece was placed in an oak tree. Jason's quest for the fleece was instigated by the duplicitous King of Iolcus, Pelias, who expected the quest to lead to Jason's death.

Maenads ("mad ones") Female followers of Dionysus, the god of wine and ecstasy. Under the influence of alcohol, the Maenads would perform orgiastic rituals, which often involved tearing animals apart. They were said to have killed Pentheus and Orpheus, both of whom had failed to honor Dionysus.

metamorphosis The transformation of one object into another. In mythology the change is usually of a human into an animal or plant. Ancient Greek mythology is full of examples of metamorphoses, often either undertaken deliberately by a god or goddess in order to fulfill a personal quest or ambition, such as Zeus turning himself into a swan in order to seduce Leda, or enacted on a mortal by a god or goddess as a form of punishment, such as when Artemis turned Actaeon into a stag. It has long been suggested that the stories of metamorphoses in early religions explains the reverse transformation: from animal worship to the worship of more humanlike deities.

Orphic Mysteries A collection of sacred verses attributed to the mythological figure Orpheus, in whose name was established the cult of Orphism. Adherents of Orphism believed in the dual nature of mankind—part divine (inherited from Dionysus) and part evil (inherited from the Titans). Only by following a strict ethical path and ascetic practices could the divine win over the evil.

Seven Against Thebes The seven champions of the Argive army that led attacks on the seven gates of the Egyptian city of Thebes. Following Oedipus' self-imposed exile from Thebes, it was agreed that his sons Eteocles and Polyneices would rule alternately. However, after the first year Eteocles refused to cede the throne to his brother. In response, Polyneices gathered an army from Argos and attacked Thebes. During the ensuing battle the brothers killed each other, and the Argive army was defeated. A family already suffering from incest and patricide now endured fratricide.

Sphinx In Greek mythology, the Sphinx was a female monster, thought by some to be the offspring of Echidna and Typhon, with a woman's head, a lion's body, and an eagle's wings. She was sent to Thebes (by Hera according to some) to avenge a past wrong-doing. She posed a riddle given to her by the Muses, and with each wrong answer a Theban was devoured. Oedipus answered the riddle correctly, and the Sphinx threw herself off a cliff and died. As reward, Oedipus was crowned King of Thebes and then married the newly widowed queen, his mother.

ADONIS

the 30-second mythology

Adonis represented the cycle

of nature: life-death-rebirth. The myths surrounding his role as lover of Aphrodite stress his great beauty and his tragic early death. Details of his parentage and birth vary, but a popular version tells how he was born after Aphrodite cursed his mother, often called Smyrna (Roman "Myrrha"), with an unnatural sexual desire for her own father. When Smyrna's father discovered his unwitting incest, he tried to kill his daughter, but the gods took pity and turned her into a tree, from which Adonis was born. Aphrodite was dazzled by the beauty of the "babe" and for protection placed him in a chest, which she asked Persephone to guard. When Persephone could not resist opening the chest and saw the child, she in turn wished to keep him for herself. Zeus adjudicated their dispute, allowing Adonis to live for four months with each goddess and four months with whomever he wished. Adonis chose Aphrodite. As a young man, Adonis remained a favorite of Aphrodite. Cosseted and naive to the dangers of hunting, he was killed by a boar, possibly sent by a jealous Ares, but was allowed to return to life for six months of each year to spend with Aphrodite.

3-SECOND MUSE
Adonis was a beautiful young man, beloved by Aphrodite and was associated with fertility.

3-MINUTE ODYSSEY
Mortal men loved by goddesses often came to unfortunate ends. Calypso despaired when Hermes, sent by Zeus, ordered her to free Odysseus, though he came to a happy end. Aurora obtained immortality for her lover Tithonus but forgot to ask for eternal youth, so that he grew old while she stayed young. In *The Golden Bough*, James Frazer turns the human Adonis into a god (of vegetation), and portrays him as an example of the myth of the dying and rising god.

RELATED MYTH
Zeus' acting as the wise adjudicator is reminiscent of Solomon, who chose between the two women who claimed an infant as their child.

3-SECOND BIOGRAPHIES
ZEUS/JUPITER
King of Olympus, god of the sky
See page 32

APOLLO
God of the sun, music, and poetry
See page 42

APHRODITE/VENUS
Goddess of love and beauty
See page 50

DIONYSUS/BACCHUS
God of wine and theater, son of Zeus
See page 56

30-SECOND TEXT
Emma Griffiths

Adonis' incandescent beauty has goddesses fighting over him.

OEDIPUS

the 30-second mythology

King Laius of Thebes learned

from an oracle that if his wife Jocasta bore a son, the son would kill him. So when Jocasta gave birth to a boy, he was left exposed in the wilderness to die or be lost forever. But the boy was found and was given to the childless King and Queen of Corinth. As an adult, Oedipus went to the Delphic Oracle to discover whether or not he was legitimate. The oracle predicted that he would kill his father and sleep with his mother. Rather than returning to Corinth, to whose king and queen he still assumed he had been born, Oedipus, horrified at the prophecy, fled. Near Thebes, he experienced the first recorded case of road rage with a traveler, who turned out to be King Laius of Thebes—Oedipus' real father. Oedipus, unaware of the person's identity, killed him and proceeded to Thebes, astride the entrance to which loomed the Sphinx, a monster with a lion's body, a woman's face, and a bird's wings. The Sphinx had posed a riddle, and while it remained unsolved, she would devour Thebans entering or leaving the city. Oedipus answered the riddle, causing the Sphinx to self-destruct. He was rewarded with the now vacant throne and the hand of the late king's wife, Jocasta. Years later the truth of who he really was and what he had done emerged.

3-SECOND MUSE
Oedipus was fated to kill his father and marry his mother, and unwittingly did so.

3-MINUTE ODYSSEY
One version of the Sphinx's riddle was: What has one voice and walks on four feet and two feet and three feet? Oedipus answered: A human being. For a baby is four-footed, an adult is two-footed, and an old person walking with a staff is three-footed. The Riddle of Man, as it is called, is known in many countries.

RELATED MYTH
Judas Iscariot is another well-known example of an unfortunate individual who was said to have killed his own father and married his mother.

3-SECOND BIOGRAPHIES
ODYSSEUS/ULYSSES
Greek hero renowned for his intelligence
See page 102

THESEUS
Greek hero who killed the Minotaur
See page 106

PERSEUS
Greek hero who killed the Gorgon Medusa
See page 108

OEDIPUS COMPLEX
Psychoanalytical term for every boy's childhood drive to kill his father in order to be able to have sex with his mother
See page 142

30-SECOND TEXT
William Hansen

Freud saw Oedipus' tragic story as a disguised expression of a universal male wish.

ANTIGONE

the 30-second mythology

Antigone was the daughter of the incestuous relationship between Oedipus and Jocasta. After her father's incest was exposed, a great war ensued, in which one of Antigone's brothers, Polyneices, led an army against Thebes, which was defended by her other brother, Eteocles. The brothers killed each other in combat, and Antigone vowed to give honorable burial to Polyneices, despite the Theban King Creon's commandment that the body be left exposed to dogs and birds. Antigone, convinced of the morality of her actions, continued with the burial plan but was captured and brought before Creon. In her defense Antigone claimed that the law of the gods trumped the law of man; Creon insisted that the laws of the state must triumph. He thereby set up the major theme of the choice between duty to the state and personal morality. He ordered Antigone to be buried alive in a cave. Antigone hanged herself just before Creon's son Haemon, who had been engaged to marry her, came to the cave. In a suicidal rage Haemon lunged at his father, then killed himself. Queen Eurydice of Thebes, wife of Creon, learning of her son's death, also killed herself, leaving Creon all alone.

3-SECOND MUSE
Antigone attempted to honor her treacherous dead brother and was accordingly sentenced to death.

3-MINUTE ODYSSEY
Sophocles' play is the first one solely about Antigone, but Euripides wrote a lost play on the topic. From a summary we learn that Creon had ordered his son Haemon to execute the girl. Instead, Haemon hid her in the countryside, where she bore his child. Later, when attending the games in Thebes, Antigone's son was recognized. Realizing that people knew Antigone was still alive, Haemon, fearing his father's wrath, killed both her and himself.

RELATED MYTH
The story of "Antigone" has been imitated by the French playwright Jean Anouilh (1943), the German dramatist Bertolt Brecht (1948), the Spanish writer María Zambrano (1967), and the Irish poet and writer Seamus Heaney (2007).

3-SECOND BIOGRAPHY
OEDIPUS
King of Thebes
Page 116

30-SECOND TEXT
Barry B. Powell

Oedipus' is the ultimate dysfunctional family in classical mythology. His daughter Antigone hangs herself after her brothers have killed each other.

ORPHEUS & EURYDICE

the 30-second mythology

Orpheus was the greatest of singer-songwriters. When he sang to the music of his lyre, not only people but also birds and beasts, trees, rivers, and rocks gathered to hear him. His beloved, Eurydice, died of a snake bite on their wedding day. Orpheus descended to the underworld and played to Hades and Persephone, pleading to have her back. The gods of death, while ordinarily implacable, were for once moved. But they allowed Eurydice to leave Hades on one condition: that he must walk on ahead and not look back to check whether she was following. Tellers of the tale have never agreed on why Orpheus, having almost reached the light of day, turned to look back and thereby see Eurydice vanish for the second and final time. There is an alternative version, according to which Orpheus was given not Eurydice but an illusion. The heartbroken poet retired to the wilderness to sing of his grief. In the end he was killed by the Maenads, wild female followers of Dionysus, who tore him to pieces and threw his head, still singing, into the River Hebrus.

3-SECOND MUSE
The most tragic love story of Greek myth is that of the great musician Orpheus and his double loss of Eurydice.

3-MINUTE ODYSSEY
The Greeks believed that Orpheus had been a real ancient poet and religious teacher. Orphism, a religion of its own, arose around his name. It centered on reincarnation and purification of the soul by ascetic practices. Some modern scholars think the original Orpheus may have been a shaman, a tribal magician who claimed that he had the ability to travel back and forth to the land of the dead.

RELATED MYTH
The katabasis, or underworld descent, is a common mythic motif. In Finnish legend the mother of the hero Lemminkäinen succeeded in bringing her son back from the underworld.

3-SECOND BIOGRAPHIES
DIONYSUS/BACCHUS
God of wine and madness
See page 56

HADES
At once god of the underworld and the underworld itself
See page 82

30-SECOND TEXT
Geoffrey Miles

The failure of Orpheus and Eurydice to enjoy their love until united in death is the ultimate tragic love story.

JASON & MEDEA

the 30-second mythology

Jason was heir to the throne,
but he was ordered by his uncle, Pelias, to
capture the Golden Fleece, which was the
gold fleece of a winged ram from Colchis, or
modern Georgia. In the *Argonautica*, the main
source of the myth, Apollonius of Rhodes tells
how, with the help of a group of heroes, called
the Argonauts, Jason reached Colchis but was
set impossible tasks by the king, Aeetes. The
king's daughter, Medea, fell in love with Jason.
When Jason promised to marry her, she used
her magic to help him win the Golden Fleece.
Later, on their return to Greece, she killed the
giant Talos, who was keeping the ship from
returning home. But after moving to Corinth,
Jason left Medea for the king's daughter, and
in the version made famous by Euripides,
Medea took revenge by killing her two children
by Jason. Jason's story fades at this point, with
a prophecy that he would be killed by a plank
from his old ship, the *Argo*. Medea left Corinth
and was welcomed in Athens by King Aegeus.
She fled Athens after trying to kill Aegeus'
stepson, Theseus, and traveled east, where her
son, Medus, founded the race of "Medes."
After her death Medea was transported to the
Elysian Fields and married Achilles.

3-SECOND MUSE
Medea's magical powers
helped Jason capture the
Golden Fleece. They
married and had two
children, but Jason later
abandoned her, and in
revenge Medea killed
their offspring.

3-MINUTE ODYSSEY
Witchcraft was
traditionally associated
with foreign, distant
places where the rules of
civilization did not apply.
Medea was the niece of
the sorceress Circe, who
beguiled Odysseus in
Homer's *Odyssey*. In some
versions Jason and Medea
visited Circe to be purified
after killing Medea's
brother Absyrtus during
their escape from Colchis.
Medea's name means
"the schemer," and
Jason's name means
"healer." Medicine and
magic were closely linked
in the ancient world.

RELATED MYTH
Like Medea, Clytemnestra took
revenge on her husband in part
because he, Agamemnon,
came home from Troy with a
mistress, Cassandra, though
also because he, like Medea,
had sacrificed their daughter
Iphigenia.

3-SECOND BIOGRAPHIES
APOLLO
Olympian god of the sun,
music, and poetry
See page 42

ACHILLES
Greatest hero of the Trojan
War, son of the nymph Thetis
See page 98

THESEUS
Heroic founder of Athens,
illegitimate son of King Aegeus
See page 106

30-SECOND TEXT
Emma Griffiths

*Medea, a woman
scorned, takes revenge
on Jason by killing
their two children.*

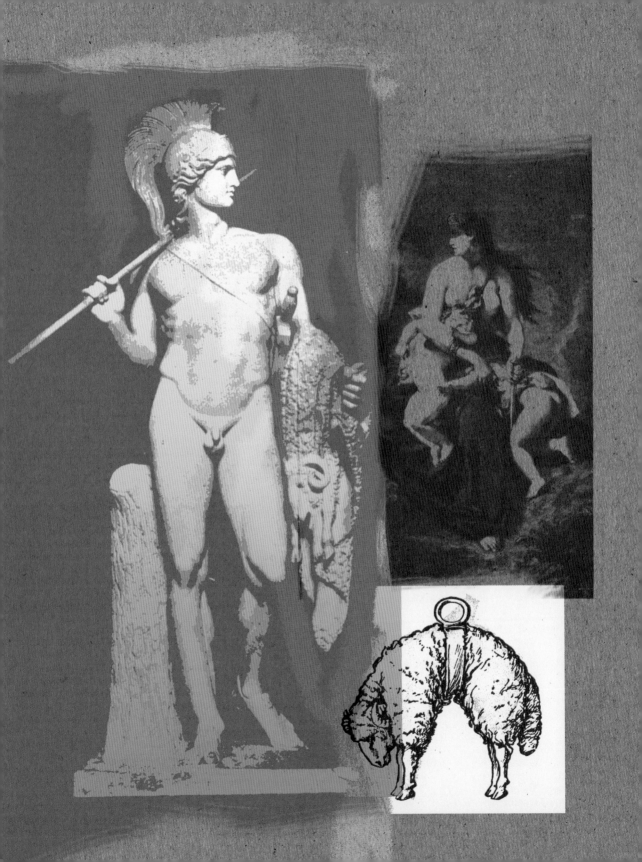

AJAX

the 30-second mythology

Ajax was second only to Achilles as the greatest Greek fighter at Troy. He was the son of Telamon and is often referred to as the Telamonian Ajax or "the greater Ajax," as opposed to fellow Greek fighter Ajax, son of Oileus, or "the lesser Ajax." Often depicted holding a gigantic shield made of seven cow-hides with a layer of bronze, Ajax was chosen by lot to meet Hector in a duel that lasted a day. The heralds eventually called a draw. When Achilles died, Ajax and Odysseus worked together to recover his body. In a rhetorical competition to determine who deserved Achilles' armor, which had been made by the god Hephaestus, Odysseus easily outshone Ajax and won the prize. Athena, Odysseus' patron god, then drove Ajax mad, causing him to kill a flock of sheep that he imagined to be the Greek leaders and judges. When he recovered and saw himself covered in sheep's blood, the humiliated Ajax went away along the loud-resounding sea and fell upon his sword. When Odysseus saw the soul of Ajax in Hades, Ajax would not speak to him and turned silently away.

3-SECOND MUSE
Ajax was a great warrior during the Trojan War. Failing to win the dead Achilles' armor, he killed himself by falling on his sword.

3-MINUTE ODYSSEY
In the mythology of Ajax, there exists not only the contrast between the mighty but ultimately fallible Ajax and the smaller but cleverer Odysseus, but also the contrast between Ajax and Achilles. While Achilles was half divine and was protected by the gods, Ajax, although descended from Zeus, was still merely human and had no gods on his side.

RELATED MYTH
The story of the big, powerful but doomed strong man is also found in the biblical stories of Goliath, slain by the boy David, and Samson, betrayed by Delilah.

3-SECOND BIOGRAPHIES
HOMER
Author of the *Iliad* and the *Odyssey*
See page 44

ACHILLES
The greatest warrior at Troy
See page 98

ODYSSEUS/ULYSSES
Greek hero, renowned for his intelligence
See page 102

30-SECOND TEXT
Barry B. Powell

Ajax's great physical might is in contrast to his occasional frailty of mind. He ultimately kills himself.

DIDO

the 30-second mythology

Dido (perhaps Phoenician for "virgin"), was the legendary founder and first Queen of Carthage, in modern Tunisia. According to archaeology, Carthage was founded sometime around 825 BCE, and Dido might have been an actual historical figure. When Dido's brother Pygmalion killed her husband, Sychaeus, Dido fled from Tyre on the eastern coast of the Mediterranean and sailed far away to the coast of North Africa. There she founded Carthage. According to Virgil's *Aeneid*, the Trojan hero Aeneas landed in Africa after fleeing the burning Troy. His mother Venus (Aphrodite) caused Dido to fall in love with the stranger, and they had a passionate relationship. Eventually, Jupiter (Zeus) sent Mercury (Hermes) to command Aeneas to proceed with his mission of founding the Roman race. As Aeneas sailed away, Dido mounted a pyre and killed herself upon it. In her dying words she cursed the Trojan and all his descendants, the Romans. From his departing ship Aeneas saw the distant glow of Dido's burning pyre. In the second and third centuries BCE, the Punic Wars, between the Romans and the Carthaginians, were the bloodiest conflicts of the ancient world.

3-SECOND MUSE
When Aeneas abandoned Dido, the beautiful Queen of Carthage, in order to fulfill his destiny of founding the Roman race, she killed herself and cursed his descendants.

3-MINUTE ODYSSEY
Aeneas saw Dido when he visited his father in the underworld. He reached out to her and apologized, but Dido turned away to join the spirit of her husband, Sychaeus. The romantic tale of Dido and Aeneas became highly popular after the Renaissance. Christopher Marlowe's first play, *Dido, Queen of Carthage*, treated the theme (1594), and it inspired many operas, including works by Francesco Cavalli (1641), Henry Purcell (1689), Niccolò Piccinni (1770), and Hector Berlioz (1860).

RELATED MYTH
Tragic love affairs are common in Greek myth, especially the stories of Jason and Medea and of Helen and Paris, on which the story of Aeneas and Dido is partly based. Odysseus, too, was detained by two demi-gods who fell in love with him: the witch Circe, with whom he spent a year, and the nymph Calypso, who kept him for seven years on her island.

3-SECOND BIOGRAPHIES
TROY
City on the Hellespont, site of the Trojan War
See page 88

AENEAS
Trojan prince, ancestor of the Romans
See page 104

VIRGIL
Roman poet, author of the *Aeneid*
See page 128

30-SECOND TEXT
Barry B. Powell

Dido is unlucky in love. Her brother murders her husband, and her lover, Aeneas, leaves her.

October 15, 70 BCE
Born in Andes, near
Mantua

42 BCE
Began to write *Eclogues*

39–38 BCE
Eclogues published

37–29 BCE
Composed the *Georgics*

29–19 BCE
Composed the *Aeneid*

19 BCE
Aeneid finished by
Lucius Varius Rufus
and Plotius Tocca (Virgil's
literary executors) at the
command of Emperor
Augustus and later
published posthumously,
despite the poet's wish
that it be burned.

September 21, 19 BCE
Died at Brundisium
(modern Brindisi)

1697
Aeneid translated by
John Dryden

1883
Eclogues translated and
illustrated by the artist
Samuel Palmer

2006
Aeneid translated by
Robert Fagles

VIRGIL

Virgil (Publius Vergilius Maro)
was one of ancient Rome's greatest poets,
master of both pastoral and epic, and a great
influence on modern Western literature. Dante
made him his guide and mentor through hell
and most of purgatory. Virgil coined some
iconic phrases, of which the best known is
omnia vincit amor (love conquers all).

After spurning a career in law, Virgil, like
Ovid, turned to poetry, at which he was very
successful despite suffering from chronic bad
health and shabby treatment from a succession
of gilded youth. He is best known for the
pastorals the *Eclogues* and the *Georgics* and
the epic the *Aeneid*. The *Eclogues* and the
Georgics are both ostensibly concerned with
aspects of life on the land but are laden with
symbolic allusions to current politics in Rome.
It was Virgil who constructed the idea of
Arcadia, the idyllic, golden pastoral paradise
idealized in the European Romantic movement,
yet which also contains Death. Virgil's position
as a gatekeeper between old and new is
supported by Book 4 of the *Eclogues*, which
Christians interpreted as prefiguring the birth
of Christ, and Book 6, which covers the myth
of Orpheus, pagan god of death and rebirth.

Virgil's greatest and most influential work
is undoubtedly the *Aeneid*. Commissioned by
Emperor Augustus, it not only was the literary
link between ancient Greek and Roman
traditions but also became the expression of
Rome's identity—part history, part myth.
Drawing inspiration from Homer's *Iliad* and
Odyssey, it is the story of Aeneas, the son
of Anchises, Prince of Troy, and the goddess
Aphrodite. When the Trojans lost the war,
Aeneas took flight with his father and a band
of supporters, inspired by a prophecy that
claimed he would found a powerful new race.
After stopping off at Carthage—where he
wooed and then spurned Dido, initiating the
Punic Wars—and Sicily, he finally settled in
Latium. After his death, Aeneas was deified.
His descendants Romulus and Remus
eventually established Rome. The Emperors
Julius and Augustus traced their ancestry
back to Aeneas, thereby linking them with
the Olympian gods and thus conferring on
Rome a divine pedigree.

PHAETHON

the 30-second mythology

3-SECOND MUSE
Phaethon, son of the sun god, died trying to emulate his father by driving his father's chariot with the sun across the sky.

3-MINUTE ODYSSEY
The warning "be careful what you wish for" is also to be found in the story of Semele, one of Zeus' lovers. Zeus' vengeful wife, Hera, tricked Semele into asking Zeus to show her how he had first appeared to Hera. Zeus had agreed to do whatever Semele, unlike Hera, asked, and although he tried to talk her out of it, he had no choice but to acquiesce. As a mortal, Semele was incinerated when Zeus revealed himself as pure light.

Together with Icarus, Phaethon ("the shining one") was the original tearaway who met a tragic end. According to one version, his mother, Klymene, told him he was the child of Helios, the sun god, but Phaethon did not believe her, so Helios promised to give him anything to prove he was his father. According to another version, Phaethon's friends doubted that he was the son of a god, so he set out to get proof. When Phaethon's father offered to grant him any wish, Phaethon asked for the reins to the chariot that Helios drove every day across the sky, a chariot pulled by winged horses. Although he tried to dissuade Phaethon from this suicidal request, Helios could not rescind the offer and could only offer vain advice to his son. The horses proved uncontrollable. As Phaethon careened through the sky, the chariot came too close to the earth and burned the lands of Africa. Zeus, afraid that the entire earth would be destroyed, struck Phaethon with a thunderbolt, and his body fell into the River Eridanos. Like Icarus, who flew too close to the sun, Phaethon serves as a warning against the recklessness of youth. Helios' granddaughter, Medea, later drove the chariot more successfully when she used it to escape from Corinth after having killed her children.

RELATED MYTH
Being unable to rescind a blessing or vow echoes the biblical story of Isaac, who was tricked into giving the blessing intended for his firstborn, Esau, to his younger son, Jacob.

3-SECOND BIOGRAPHIES
ZEUS/JUPITER
King of Olympus, god of the sky
See page 32

ICARUS
Son of Daedalus, who flew too close to the sun
See page 132

30-SECOND TEXT
Emma Griffiths

Phaethon's youthful exuberance proves his undoing. The story tallies with the Greek ideal of moderation.

ICARUS

the 30-second mythology

Minos, the King of Crete, had imprisoned the brilliant inventor Daedalus, who was kept within the labyrinth that he himself had built at the king's request. Considering his options, Daedalus ruled out escape by land or sea, since Crete was an island and Minos controlled the seas. However, there was always a third option: the air. So Daedalus collected feathers and arranged them in winglike configurations, binding them together with twine and wax. He made one set for himself and another for his son, Icarus. When it was time to escape, Daedalus warned his son not to fly too low, where the humidity might weigh down his wings, or too high, where the sun might melt their wax. Then the two arose in flight, son following father. Seeing them, a few people were amazed and assumed they were gods. Icarus, however, became so exhilarated by the experience that he soared ever higher, until the sun melted the wax of his wings, and he plummeted to his death into the waters below. The sea in which he drowned became known as the Icarian Sea, and the nearby island where the grieving father buried his son was renamed Icaria.

3-SECOND MUSE
Icarus was a Greek youth whose artificial wings, held together by wax, disintegrated when he flew too close to the sun.

3-MINUTE ODYSSEY
The Icarian Sea probably got its name from the nearby island of Icaria, but how Icaria acquired its name is anybody's guess. According to the Icarus legend, the sea and the island were so called because Icarus drowned in the one and was interred on the other. Such etiological motifs, which sometimes appear at the conclusion of traditional narratives, typically trace a feature of the world to a single event in the past.

RELATED MYTH
Humans in mythology who achieve the dream of flight less often employ their own synthetic wings than hitch a ride on a large bird. The earliest example is Etana (Mesopotamia).

3-SECOND BIOGRAPHY
PHAETHON
Tragic youth who drove the sun's chariot
See page 130

30-SECOND TEXT
William Hansen

Icarus discovers, to his cost, that pride leads to a fall.

ACTAEON

the 30-second mythology

Actaeon was part of a famous dynasty. His mother, Autonoe, was the daughter of the Theban hero Cadmus, and his father was Aristaeus, a son of the god Apollo. Actaeon was educated by the centaur Chiron and became a famous hunter, sometimes said to be a companion of the goddess Artemis. In the main version of the myth, as told by Callimachus and Ovid, Actaeon offended the goddess by inadvertently coming upon her naked in the woods. Other versions claim that he boasted that he could hunt better than Artemis or that he was a suitor for the princess Semele, whom Zeus loved. Whatever the offense, the punishment was the same: Artemis turned him into a stag and drove his hounds mad so they tore him to pieces on Mount Cithaeron. On the same mountain Pentheus was torn to pieces for having insulted the god Dionysus, and the baby Oedipus was abandoned just after birth. In some tellings of the myth the hounds were so grief stricken when they realized what they had done that Chiron made a statue of Actaeon to console them.

3-SECOND MUSE
A Greek mythological hunter who, having offended Artemis, was transformed into a stag and torn apart by his own hounds.

3-MINUTE ODYSSEY
Metamorphosis from human to animal is a common motif in myth. Callisto was turned into a bear after she had broken a vow to Artemis, and was then hunted until she died. Although many transformations were punishments, they could also be an act of salvation as when Procne and Philomela were turned into birds as they fled from Tereus, or when Zeus turned Io into a cow to hide her from the jealous rage of Hera.

RELATED MYTH
In the Ugaritic myth of Daniel and Aqhat, the goddess Anat killed the hunter Aqhat when he offended her by refusing a trade.

3-SECOND BIOGRAPHIES
ZEUS/JUPITER
King of Olympus, god of the sky
See page 32

ARTEMIS/DIANA
Daughter of Zeus and Leto, virgin goddess of the hunt
See page 46

DIONYSUS/BACCHUS
God of wine and theater, son of Zeus,
See page 56

30-SECOND TEXT
Emma Griffiths

As punishment for having dared see her naked, Actaeon the hunter is turned by Artemis into the hunted.

LEGACY

complex In psychology, a termed coined by C. G. Jung to describe a set of emotionally charged experiences caused by either a childhood experience (Freud) or an innate archetype (Jung). The complex can express itself in many ways, usually symbolically. Mental health requires the recognition of the complex. Eventually, the term was used by Freudians exclusively, as in Oedipus complex.

hypersexuality Sexual activity in either men or women that affects normal social functioning or causes distress. The term replaces the traditional, mythologically rooted terms "nymphomania" and "satyriasis."

neurotic A person suffering from a neurosis, which in psychoanalytic terms means an unconscious emotional conflict, going back to childhood, that manifests itself in adulthood in ways that overtly have nothing to do with childhood but that are in fact disguised expressions of unresolved sexual and emotional tensions. Traditionally, neuroses are treated through analysis.

nymphomania Term that used to be applied to what was considered excessive sexuality in women. It then came to be seen as a symptom of a larger personality disorder. It is now called hypersexuality or just sex addiction.

Oedipal stage In Freud's stages of pyschosexual development, the Oedipal (or phallic) stage occurs between the ages of three and five, and describes the stage at which children become possessive of the parent of the opposite sex, while seeing the parent of the same sex as a rival. Freud considered the Oedipal stage—a term he used for girls as well as for boys—as the key one for the development of personality and as the key, though by no means the only, source of adult psychological problems.

personality disorder Any one of a range of disorders which keep an individual from dealing flexibly and sensibly with the varying situations that life presents. Those suffering from a personality disorder react rigidly and unbendingly to situations. The major disorders include paranoia, schizophrenia, histrionics, and anti-social behavior. A person may suffer from more than one disorder.

pre-Oedipal stage Freud's unbending view was that the key stage of psychosexual development was the Oedipal stage. His once-close disciple and even heir, Otto Rank, came to maintain that the key stage is in fact pre-Oedipal, or the stage right after birth. For Freud, the fundamental relationship in the Oedipal stage is that between a child and the parent of the same sex. For Rank, the fundamental relationship in the pre-Oedipal stage is that between a child, boy or girl, and the mother. Where for Freud the child seeks to replace the parent of the same sex, for Rank the child seeks to remain united with the mother in the womb. The trauma that determines one's personality comes not at age three but at birth. Freudians today, while still considering Rank a heretic, have long since come to give at least as much importance to the pre-Oedipal stage as to the Oedipal one.

satyriasis Term once used for the male counterpart to nymphomania. As in nymphomania, excessive sexuality was seen as a symptom of a broader psychological malady. This term, too, has now been replaced by hypersexuality or sex addiction.

NARCISSISM

the 30-second mythology

Narcissus was an exceptionally attractive youth who, rejecting both males and females, was punished by one spurned male by being made to fall in love with his own reflection in the water. Narcissus had no understanding of reflection and so did not realize that he was beholding only a mirror of himself and not his actual self. Unable to grasp hold of his reflection yet unable to break the attraction, he withered away and died. He was turned into a flower, the narcissus. The term "narcissism" refers to excessive self-absorption and obliviousness to others. The term was coined by the English physician and pioneering sexologist Havelock Ellis to refer to excessive masturbation but was expanded and enriched into a psychological state by the far more theoretical Sigmund Freud. "Healthy narcissism" is the common current term for sufficient attention to oneself and not just to others. Narcissism as a personality disorder refers to preoccupation with oneself at the expense of others. For Freud, narcissism as an illness is the carrying of healthy narcissism to an extreme.

30-SECOND TEXT
Robert A. Segal

3-SECOND MUSE
Narcissism is the name for the state of persons excessively absorbed with themselves. It is more extreme than sheer vanity, pride, or self-confidence.

3-MINUTE ODYSSEY
The source of narcissism remains moot. One common psychoanalytic explanation is the denial of love during early years. Unloved as a child, the adult narcissist in turn can feel no love for others. Narcissists are incapable of empathy. They are often charming on the surface but in fact are manipulative, cunning, and deceitful. The concept of narcissism has been applied to whole cultures, most famously to contemporary America by Christopher Lasch in *The Culture of Narcissism* (1979).

While Narcissus' self-love is the result of a curse, Freud offers a scientific explanation of the phenomenon generally.

OEDIPUS COMPLEX

the 30-second mythology

3-SECOND MUSE
"Oedipus complex" is
Freud's name for the drive
in all boys from three to
five to kill their fathers in
order to have sex with
their mothers.

3-MINUTE ODYSSEY
Freud stalwartly made the
Oedipus complex the heart
of his psychology. But
since his day, the focus
of even mainstream
psychoanalysis has shifted
from the Oedipal stage,
which for Freud centered
on the conflict between
sons and fathers, to the
pre-Oedipal stage, which
focuses on the relations,
by no means hostile,
between children and
mothers. At the same
time the term "Oedipus
complex" has come to be
applied to females as well
as to males. The term
"Electra complex" is no
longer used.

The subject of, above all,
Sophocles' play *Oedipus Rex* (*Oedipus the
King*), Oedipus is perhaps the most famous
human figure from Greek mythology, though
his fame stems partly from the appropriation
of his saga by Freud. As a victim of a curse on
his house, King Laius of Thebes was warned
that if he fathered a son, the son would one
day kill him. Laius accepted the prophecy and
instructed a servant to kill the infant, whose
conception had stemmed from an episode of
drunkenness and so loss of self-control. Laius
thought that, by having his son killed, he could
outwit the prophecy. Alas, Oedipus was saved,
was raised elsewhere, and as an adult fulfilled
the prophecy, which now included incest with
his mother. Even though Oedipus was seemingly
the victim of Fate, which he, like his father,
tried vainly to circumvent, Freud made him
the victimizer. For Freud, as presented in *The
Interpretation of Dreams* (1900), Oedipus, as
an adult, fulfilled the childhood drive in all
males: to kill their fathers in order to secure
sexual access to their mothers. The "Oedipus
complex" is normal in childhood but neurotic
when carried on into adulthood, even if never
outwardly fulfilled.

3-SECOND BIOGRAPHIES
OEDIPUS
King of Thebes; he killed his
father and married his mother
See page 116

SOPHOCLES
Greek playwright, author of
Oedipus Rex
See page 146

30-SECOND TEXT
Robert A. Segal

*All boys naturally
want to kill their
fathers and sleep
with their mothers ...
so says Freud.*

ELECTRA COMPLEX

the 30-second mythology

3-SECOND MUSE
"Electra complex" names the stage of development in which all girls fantasize killing their mother in order to get sexual access to their father.

3-MINUTE ODYSSEY
The term "Electra complex" fits the phenomenon it names less well than the term "Oedipus complex" fits its phenomenon. Whereas the mythological character Oedipus actually killed his father and then proceeded to marry his mother, Electra was not the one who killed her mother, and her father was already dead. Oedipus did the very things that, consciously, he least wanted to do, whereas Electra did consciously want her mother dead.

In Greek mythology, Electra was the daughter of King Agamemnon and Queen Clytemnestra. Of her siblings, the most important were her elder sister, Iphigenia, and her brother Orestes. Agamemnon was the leader of the Greek army that fought at Troy. While Agamemnon was away, Clytemnestra took a lover, Aegisthus. Together, they killed Agamemnon upon his triumphant return home. Clytemnestra hated him because he had sacrificed Iphigenia so that the Greek forces could get the wind needed to sail to Troy. She also hated him because he had come home with a mistress, Cassandra. Electra sided with her father despite his actions, and she persuaded Orestes to kill their mother. It was not Freud but his rival, Carl Gustav Jung, who coined the term "complex" and later, in 1913, the specific instance "Electra complex," by which he meant the universal drive in girls from three to five to seek sex with their fathers and to kill their mothers, who stand in the way. Freud took the term complex from Jung and coined the term "Oedipus complex," to which the Electra complex was meant to be the female counterpart. Once Freud and Jung split, Freud abandoned the term Electra complex and preferred to use "Oedipus complex" for both sexes.

3-SECOND BIOGRAPHY
OEDIPUS
King of Thebes; he killed his father and married his mother
See page 116

30-SECOND TEXT
Robert A. Segal

All girls naturally want to kill their mothers and sleep with their fathers ... so says Freud and so originally said Jung as well.

495 BCE
Born at Colonus near
Athens, the son of a
wealthy merchant

468 BCE
Won first prize at the
Athens Dionysia festival,
defeating Aeschylus

444 BCE
Ajax first staged

442 BCE
Wrote *Antigone*

409 BCE
Wrote *Philoctetes*
and *Electra*

406 BCE
Wrote *Oedipus Coloneus*
(*Oedipus at Colonus*)

405 BCE
Died

401 BCE
Oedipus Coloneus
first staged

1954
Oedipus the King
translated by David
Grene; *Oedipus at
Colonus* translated by
Robert Fitzgerald;
Antigone translated by
Elizabeth Wyckoff

1954
The Three Theban Plays:
*Antigone, Oedipus the
King, Oedipus at Colonus*
translated by Robert
Fagles

PYGMALION EFFECT

the 30-second mythology

3-SECOND MUSE
The term "Pygmalion effect," while named after a sculptor whose sculpture comes to life, refers to the change that others' expectations can have on their subjects.

3-MINUTE ODYSSEY
In the *Metamorphoses* Ovid describes the transformations of humans and also nymphs into animals and plants. The transformation of Pygmalion's sculpture into a living female, through the power of love, is typically Ovidian. The rather less romantic Robert Merton (1910–2003) coined the term "self-fulfilling prophecy," by which the "Pygmalion effect" is now far better known. His example is of a solvent bank that goes bankrupt as a result of false rumors of its insolvency, rumors that lead customers to withdraw their money.

In the *Metamorphoses* Ovid tells the story of a sculptor named Pygmalion, who, revolted by the pervasiveness of prostitutes, forswore sex and lived as a celibate. But he sculpted an ivory statue of a beautiful virgin and fell in love with the statue. When he returned home from a festival to Venus, he kissed the statue, which, thanks to Venus, immediately came to life. The link to the term "Pygmalion effect," coined by the American sociologist Robert Merton, is tricky. Well before George Bernard Shaw's most famous play, *Pygmalion*, appeared in 1912, there had been English comedies in which a married sculptor created a beautiful female that then came alive. Not his but her name became Pygmalion. Writing not a comedy but a comic satire on the rigidity of class, Shaw made Pygmalion, renamed Eliza Doolittle, a living person from the start. The transformation in his play is not from statue to living being but from cockney flower girl to aristocrat. The transformation succeeds less because of what she does and more because of her acceptance as an aristocrat by high society. The "effect" means the effect that others' expectations, negative as well as positive, can have on their subjects.

3-SECOND BIOGRAPHY
OVID
Greek playwright, author of *Metamorphoses*
See page 70

30-SECOND TEXT
Robert A. Segal

The notion of "living up to other people's expectations" is much different from the original myth of Pygmalion.

APPENDICES

RESOURCES

BOOKS

Ancient Goddesses: The Myths and the Evidence
Lucy Goodison and Christine Morris
(University of Wisconsin Press, 1999)

Anthology of Classical Myth: Primary Sources in Translation
Stephen M. Trzaskoma et al.
(Hackett, 2004)

Aphrodite
Monica S. Cyrino
(Routledge, 2010)

Apollo
Fritz Graf
(Routledge, 2009)

Apollodorus' Library and Hyginus' Fabulae: Two Handbooks of Greek Mythology
R. Scott Smith and Stephen M. Trzaskoma
(Hackett, 2007)

Art and Myth in Ancient Greece
Thomas H. Carpenter
(Thames & Hudson, 1991)

Athena
Susan Deacy
(Routledge, 2008)

The Cambridge Companion to Greek Mythology
Roger D. Woodard (ed.)
(Cambridge University Press, 2007)

Classical Myth (7th edn)
Barry B. Powell
(Prentice Hall, 2011)

Classical Mythology: A Guide to the Mythical World of the Greeks and Romans
William Hansen
(Oxford University Press, 2005)

Classical Mythology: A Very Short Introduction
Helen Morales
(Oxford University Press, 2007)

Classical Mythology in English Literature: A Critical Anthology
Geoffrey Miles (ed.)
(Routledge, 1999)

The Complete World of Greek Mythology
Richard Buxton
(Thames & Hudson, 2004)

The Dictionary of Classical Mythology
Pierre Grimal, trans. A. R. Maxwell-Hyslop
(Blackwell, 1986)

Dionysus
Richard Seaford
(Routledge, 2006)

Greek Mythology, An Introduction
Fritz Graf, trans. Thomas Marier
(Johns Hopkins University Press, 1993)

A Handbook of Greek Mythology
Herbert J. Rose
(Methuen, first edn 1928; sixth edn, 1958)

Heracles
Emma Stafford
(Routledge, 2011)

Medea
Emma Griffiths
(Routledge, 2006)

The Meridian Handbook of Classical Mythology (originally *Crowell's Handbook of Classical Mythology* [Crowell, 1970])
Edward Tripp
(Meridian, 1974)

The Mirror of the Gods: How Renaissance Artists Rediscovered the Pagan Gods
Malcolm Bull
(Oxford University Press, 2005)

The Modern Construction of Myth
Andrew Von Hendy
(Indiana University Press, 2002)

Myth: Critical Concepts in Literary and Cultural Studies (4 vols.)
Robert A. Segal (ed.)
(Routledge 2007)

Myth: A Very Short Introduction
Robert A. Segal
(Oxford University Press, 2004)

Myths of the Greeks and Romans (rev. edn)
Michael Grant
(Penguin 1995)

The Myths of Rome
Timothy P. Wiseman
(University of Exeter Press, 2004)

The Nature of Greek Myths
Geoffrey S. Kirk
(Penguin, 1974)

Oedipus
Lowell Edmunds
(Routledge, 2006)

Perseus
Daniel Ogden
(Routledge, 2008)

Prometheus
Carol Dougherty
(Routledge, 2006)

RESOURCES

The Rise of Modern Mythology 1680–1860
Burton Feldman and Robert D. Richardson
(Indiana University Press, 1972)

Roman Myths
Michael Grant
(Penguin, 1973)

The Routledge Handbook of Greek Mythology (based on H. J. Rose's *A Handbook of Greek Mythology*)
Robin Hard
(Routledge, 2004)

A Short Introduction to Classical Myth
Barry B. Powell
(Prentice Hall, 2002)

The Survival of the Pagan Gods: The Mythological Tradition and its Place in Renaissance Humanism and Art
Jean Seznec
(Princeton University Press, 1953)

The Uses of Greek Mythology
Ken Dowden
(Routledge, 1992)

Zeus
Ken Dowden
(Routledge, 2006)

WEB SITES & LIBRARY COLLECTIONS

The Bryn Mawr Classical Review at http://ccat.sas-upenn.edu/bmcr/arch.html
Richard Hamilton and James J. O'Donnell (eds). A searchable archive of recent publications pertaining to the classical world. The leading review journal of classical studies.

Lexicon Iconographicum Mythologiae Classicae (*LIMC*) (Zurich, 1981–99). Massive multi-volume compilation of every representation of every myth, with scholarly commentary in several languages but mostly English. The single leading resource for the study of myth and art in the ancient world, invaluable but available only in research libraries.

The Ovid Collection at the University of Virginia. http://etext.lib.virginia.edu/latin/ovid/

The Perseus Project, ed. Gregory R. Crane et al., has thousands of links to texts, works of art, maps, lexica, and other aids to understanding myth and the classical world. http://www.perseus.tufts.edu

Theoi Greek Mythology: Exploring Mythology in Classical Literature and Art. http://www.theoi.com/

NOTES ON CONTRIBUTORS

Viv Croot is a writer with a particular interest in popularizing specialist subjects. Her fascination with the literature of classical Greece focuses on the *Iliad* and the *Odyssey* and their influence on the Western literary tradition. She is co-author of *Troy: Homer's Iliad Retold* (Barnes & Noble, 2004).

Susan Deacy is Senior Lecturer in Greek History and Literature at Roehampton University, London. Her work on Athena has led to an exploration of the range of figures with whom this especially adaptable of ancient religious personages is connected. Deacy is editor of the "Gods and Heroes of the Ancient World" series for Routledge, and author of publications, including *A Traitor to her Sex? Athena the Trickster* (forthcoming, Oxford University Press).

Emma Griffiths is a Lecturer in Greek at the University of Manchester. She has published on many aspects of Greek mythology and drama, and is currently working on a book about children in Greek tragedy.

William Hansen is Professor Emeritus of Classical Studies and Folklore and formerly co-director of the program in Mythology Studies at Indiana University, Bloomington. His books include *Anthology of Ancient Greek Popular Literature* (Indiana University Press, 1998), *Ariadne's Thread: A Guide to International Tales Found in Classical Literature* (Cornell University Press, 2002), and *Classical Mythology: A Guide to the Mythical World of the Greeks and Romans* (Oxford University Press, 2005).

Geoffrey Miles is Senior Lecturer in English at Victoria University of Wellington, New Zealand, with a special interest in the transformations of the classical world and classical myth in English literature. He is the editor of *Classical Mythology in English Literature* (1999), and co-author of *The Snake-Haired Muse* (2011), a study of the use of myth by the New Zealand poet James K. Baxter.

Barry B. Powell is Halls-Bascom Professor of Classics Emeritus at University of Wisconsin–Madison. His books include *Classical Myth* (Prentice Hall, 2011), *Writing: Theory and History of the Technology of Civilization* (Wiley/Blackwell, 2009), and *Homer and the Origin of the Greek Alphabet* (Cambridge University Press, 1991). He is co-author (with Ian Morris) of *A New Companion to Homer* (Brill, 1997), and *The Greeks: History, Culture, and Society* (Prentice Hall, 2009).

Robert A. Segal is Sixth Century Chair in Religious Studies at the University of Aberdeen, Scotland. He is a leading authority on approaches to myth and is the author of *Myth: A Very Short Introduction* (Oxford University Press, 2004) and *Theorizing about Myth* (University of Massachusetts Press, 1999). He also edits the "Theorists of Myth" series for Routledge.

INDEX

ACKNOWLEDGMENTS

PICTURE CREDITS
The publisher would like to thank the following
individuals and organizations for their kind
permission to reproduce the images in this
book. Every effort has been made to acknowledge
the pictures. However we apologize if there
are any omissions.

Ian W. Scott: 20.